VIRGINIA TITHABLES

From Burned Record Counties

Buckingham	1773-1774
Gloucester	1770-1771
	1774-1775
Hanover	1763 and 1770
James City	1768-1769
Stafford	1768 and 1773

Compiled by

Robert F. Woodson

Isobel B. Woodson

Published by

Isobel B. Woodson

September 1970

Copyright 1970
By: Isobel B. Woodson

Copyright Transferred 1982
To: The Rev. Silas Emmett Lucas, Jr.

All rights reserved. No part of this publication may be reproduced,
stored in a retrieval system, transmitted in any form,
posted on to the web in any form or by any means
without the prior written permission of the publisher.

Please direct all correspondence and orders to:

www.southernhistoricalpress.com
or
**SOUTHERN HISTORICAL PRESS, Inc.
PO BOX 1267
375 West Broad Street
Greenville, SC   29601
southernhistoricalpress@gmail.com**

ISBN #0-89308-306-2

Printed in the United States of America

IN MEMORIAM

ROBERT F. WOODSON

1906 - 1967

EXPLANATIONS

Spelling and Abreviations used herein are the same as those shown in the tithable lists. The lack of standardization was due largely to the various commissioners, who prepared the list, having different opinions on what constituted correct spelling or abreviation.

Gloucester County tithables sometimes show "Ware", "Abingdon", and "Petsworth" without other enlightening entries. They were parishes in Gloucester by those names.

* - Names appearing with this symbol were copied from the index to the 1770 Tax Book of Gloucester in which some pages were missing.

Kingston Parish often appears in the Gloucester lists. This parish was detached from that county in 1791 to form the present county of Mathews.

The Hanover County tax list for 1763 frequently shows another year in parenthesis. The meaning of such entries is not clear, however, they suggest that the land was owned by the tithable person in the county on the date shown.

A person whose name is indented was a titable in the household of the person listed above, whose name is not indented.

_____, name omitted.

( ) - record difficult to decipher or mutilated.

Q.R. - abreviation for Quit Rent.

N.P. - abreviation for new patent.

FOREWORD

The court records of Northumberland are the earliest in the Northern Neck. Here ancestors who were driven from the Isle of Kent by the Early Marylanders mixed with those coming up the Bay from the earlier settlements along the James and the York. "Roundheads" and "Cavaliers"--they were all here. At first they were traders in furs, corn and other goods. Later they sought to acquire lands and clear fields to raise tobacco and other crops. They were a tough and ambitious lot.

One of the first to come was John Mottrom, who established a trading post at the mouth of the Coan River--then called Chickacoane. He arrived about the time the Ark and the Dove deposited the Marylanders across the Potomac at St. Mary's. In this area a considerable settlement soon arose to the extent that John Mottrom travelled to Jamestown in 1645, as their unofficial representative. In 1648, the county of Northumberland was officially formed, and John Mottrom was named as the first elected Burgess.

Perhaps the two most important pages in our records provides us with the holograph signatures of one hundred of our oldest residents. The occasion was the Oath of Allegiance in April 1652, when they promised "to be true and faithful to the Commonwealth of England as it is now established without King or House of Lordes."

In these early years the inhabitants of Northumberland gradually prospered. They built good homes, established productive plantations, and generally had few deterants to their economy until the Revolutionary War.

Though no major engagements took place on our shores during the Revolution we were subjected to raids by the British Navy. Many homes were destroyed and possessions carried off. Again during the War of 1812, even greater destruction was perpetrated by the British. During the Civil War the same misfortune overtook us--this time from the North. Evidence of all of this is to be found in the pages of our excellently kept county records, most of which have been restored.

Mrs. Bayne Palmer O'Brien, supplies in this census of 1850, an important key for the better use of our public records. In that year for the first time we are given names of parents, their children, others living in the home, their ages, etc.. This information is an invaluable clue to those engaged in historical research. Mrs. O'Brien is to be congratulated for this timely aid for all who search the records of Northumberland.

J. Motley Booker, M. D., President

Northumberland County Historical Society

BIBLIOGRAPHY

Buckingham County. Tithables 1773-1774. Virginia State Library. Accession No. 20238.

Gloucester County. Tax Accounts. 1770-1771. Virginia State Library Accession No. 21341.

Gloucester County. Tithables. Kingston Parish. 1774-1775. Virginia State Library Accession No. 20998. County Records.

Hanover County. Rent Roll 1763. Public Record Office, London, England. A.O. 13/30. Folder G II. Endorsed. "A True and Perfect Rent Roll of all the Lands in the County of Hanover paying Quitrents to His Majesty for the year One Thousand Seven Hundred and Sixty (three) so far as I (am) able to discover." Sheriff of the said county am 176___ (The date appears on the individual pages.) From the Loyalist Claim of Samuel Gist.

Hanover County. 1770. This list was copied from the Virginia Genealogist, Volume 5-6, 1961-62. Edited by John Frederick Dorman, and with his permission. "St. Martin's Parish Hanover County Tax List, 1770. A List of Tithes, Land & Wheel Carriages in St. Martin's Parish for 1770" is among the Overton Papers (Box 1, folder 25) at the College of William and Mary. It is printed with the permission of the Librarian.

James City County. Tax Book. 1768-1769. Virginia State Library. County Records.

Stafford County. Rental. 1768. Virginia State Library Accession No. 21191.

Stafford County. Rental. 1773. Virginia State Library Accession No. 21192.

INTRODUCTION

The migration of families within Virginia and to newer lands in the south and west during the late colonial period and the years of the American Revolution has often made it difficult to establish the place of origin of these pioneers. Where the usual court records exist it may be possible to locate the former home and eventually to trace their ancestry. Many counties in Virginia, however, have lost their court records as a result of fire or war. In these counties it is difficult even to determine who were the residents before the Revolutionary War.

In the Virginia State Library there are a few colonial tithable lists and quit rent rolls for various counties. This volume contains the names from extant lists for the late colonial period of five counties for which all or most court records are no longer extant. For these "burned record counties" the lists published herein provide the names of the property owners and therefore serve as a sort of census. The five counties are Buckingham, Gloucester, Hanover, James City, and Stafford.

The law under which these tax lists were created was an Act of the Virginia Assembly of October 1748 (W. W. Hening, The Statutes at Large ... of Virginia, v. 6, pp. 40-44) which declared that the following persons were subject to payment of tax:

    All male persons sixteen years of age and upwards
    Negro, mulatto and Indian women of the same age, except
        Tributary Indians
    Wives of free Negroes, mulattos and Indians, except as
        above exempted

The Governor and his domestic servants, the President, masters and scholars of the College of William and Mary and their domestic servants, any beneficed minister and constables while serving in office were exempted from paying the poll tax.

In addition, every land owner owed yearly to the government quit rent for the land he held. In the case of Stafford County the rent was payable to the Proprietor of the Northern Neck, Lord Fairfax.

The responsibility for the payment of the tax was on the head of the household where the taxable person resided. In this volume the names of some of the tithables are indented to show that the tax was payable by the one under whose name he is listed.

There are instances in which the same name appears more than once in a county record for the same year. In such cases there was more than one person of the name in the county.

The original spelling has been used and the notations are given just as they appeared on the lists. There is no uniformity to the lists of the several counties included herein or even to the lists of various dates of one county. The Buckingham County lists do not show land holdings; the Stafford County list is concerned only with land.

When two men of the same surname are listed together, relationship (usually father and son) may be presumed. When land is shown a comparison of the entry with the land tax lists of

1782 may suggest that the colonial taxpayer was the father of one or more persons named in 1782 and reference to earlier land patents may provide other suggestions of family relationship.

The Hanover County tithable list of 1763 frequently contains a date beside the statement of acreage owned. The meaning of this date is not stated on the list. In all likelihood, however, it shows the period from which quit rent was due and therefore serves to indicate that the taxpayer was resident on that land some years previous to 1763.

A careful study of the information in this book when combined with a cautious but imaginative approach to a genealogical problem may produce unexpected rewards.

John Frederick Dorman

Washington, D.C.
September 1970

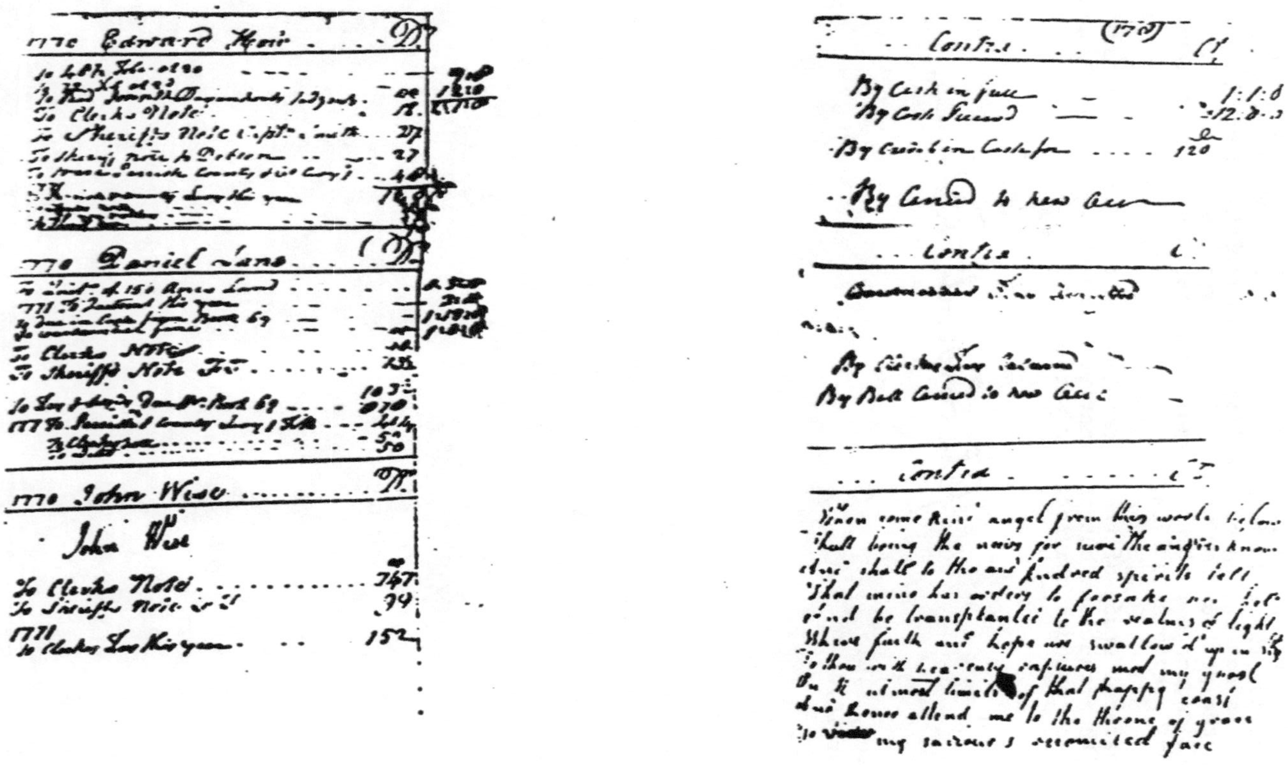
1770 John Wise

John Wise

To Clerks Note

By Cash in full

Contra

Typical page from the Gloucester County tax took 1770-1771

Name	County	Year	Tith-ables	Acres
ABBOT. George	Buckingham	1773	1	
ABBOT, George	Buckingham	1774	1	
ABNEY, Mary	Hanover	1763		600
ACCOKICK COMPANY	Stafford	1768		2796
ACRE, Joshua	Hanover	1763		200
ADAMS, Christopher (Kingston Par.)	Gloucester	1774	4	
ADAMS, Christopher (Kingston Par.)	Gloucester	1775	4	
ADAMS, James	Hanover	1763		100
ADAMS, Peter	Hanover	1763		115
ADAMS, Richard	James City	1768		
ADAMS, Zachariah (Kingston Parish)	Gloucester	1774	3	
ADAMS, Zachariah (Kingston Parish)	Gloucester	1775	3	
ADCOCK, Anderson	Buckingham	1773	2	
ADCOCK, Anderson	Buckingham	1774	2	
ADCOCK, Edmund, see Stimson, John				
ADCOCK, George	Buckingham	1773	3	
ADCOCK, George	Buckingham	1774	3	
ADCOCK, John	Buckingham	1773	3	
ADCOCK, John	Buckingham	1774	4	
ADCOCK, John	Buckingham	1773	4	
Adcock, Joseph				
ADCOCK, John	Buckingham	1774	4	
Adcock, Joseph				
ADCOCK, Joseph	Buckingham	1773	4	
ADCOCK, Joseph	Buckingham	1774	5	
ADCOCK, Joseph	Buckingham	1774	1	
ADCOCK. Joseph, see Adcock, John				
ADCOCK, Joseph Junr.	Buckingham	1773		
Levy free, 1 Negro				
ADDIE, William	Stafford	1773		750
ADDISON, John	Stafford	1773		200
Now Thownshend Dade's				
ADDISON. John	Stafford	1768		200
ADDISON. John, see Young, William				
ADIE, William	Stafford	1768		750
ADKINS, Peter	Buckingham	1774	3	
Hillard, John				
AGEE, Anthony	Buckingham	1773	1	
AGEE, Anthony	Buckingham	1773	2	
Agee, William				
AGEE, Anthony	Buckingham	1774	3	
Agee, William				
Agee, Joshua				
AGEE, Anthony, Junr.	Buckingham	1774	1	
AGEE, Isaac	Buckingham	1773	1	
AGEE, Isaac	Buckingham	1774	1	
AGEE, James, Senr.	Buckingham	1773	4	
Agee, James, Jr.	Buckingham	1774		
AGEE, James, Senr.	Buckingham	1774	5	
Agee, James, Jr.				
AGEE, John	Buckingham	1773	1	
AGEE, John	Buckingham	1774	1	
AGEE, Joshua, see Agee, Anthony				
AGEE, Mathew	Buckingham	1773	1	
AGEE, Matthew	Buckingham	1774	2	
Ligon, Jno.				
AGEE, Wm., see Agee, Anthony				
AKERS, John	Buckingham	1773	1	
AKERS, John	Buckingham	1774	1	
AKERS, Wm.	Buckingham	1773	1	

Name	County	Year	Tithables	Acres
AKERS, Wm.	Buckingham	1774	1	
AKERS, William Jr.	Buckingham	1773	2	
AKERS, William Jr.	Buckingham	1774	2	
ALCROFT, George	James City	1768		
ALEXANDER, Charles	Stafford	1768		2500
ALEXANDER, Charles lives in Fairfax	Stafford	1773		2500
ALEXANDER, John	Stafford	1768		4230
ALEXANDER, John Ditto 750 A. of Dunn from King George Co.	Stafford	1773		4230
ALEXANDER, Morgan	Gloucester	1770		
ALEXANDER, Morgan	Gloucester	1771		
ALEXR. (sic), Wm. see Woodson, John				
ALGER, Dennis	Gloucester	1770		
ALLASON, Wm., see Hooe, Ann				
ALLEN, Benjamin	Hanover	1763	(1762)95	
ALLEN, David, Este. insolvent	James City	1768	1	
ALLEN, Elebeth Mrs.	Buckingham	1773	3	
ALLEN, Elizabeth Coleman, Benja.	Buckingham	1774	4	
ALLEN, Ellinor	James City	1768	5	650
ALLEN, Ellinor	James City	1769	3	650
ALLEN, George Hunt Kidd, Wm.	Buckingham	1773	12	
ALLEN, George Hunt Kidd, Wm.	Buckingham	1774	12	
ALLEN, Hudson	James City	1768	6	175
ALLEN, Hudson	James City	1769	5	175
ALLEN, Isham	James City	1768	1	
ALLEN, Isham	James City	1769	1	
ALLEN, James	Hanover	1763		432
ALLEN, James	James City	1769	1	
ALLEN, James	Stafford	1773		443
ALLEN, John	James City	1768	1	
ALLEN, John	James City	1769	4	
ALLEN, John Allen, Kinsman	Buckingham	1773	2	
ALLEN, John Kinsman, Allen (sic)	Buckingham	1774	2	
ALLEN, John, Exrs.	Stafford	1768		300
ALLEN, John, Exrs.	Stafford	1773		300
ALLEN, Jones	James City	1769	3	250
ALLEN, Julius	James City	1769	3	
ALLEN, Keziah	James City	1769	1	
ALLEN, Kinsman, see Allen, John				
ALLEN, Rebecca	James City	1768	8	425
ALLEN, Rebecca	James City	1769	8	425
ALLEN, William, Exrs.	Stafford	1768		905
ALLEN, William	James City	1769	9	200
ALLEN, Wm., see Walter, William				
ALLEN, Wm. Capn.	James City	1768	9	200
ALLEN, Wm. Hunt	Buckingham	1773	9	
ALLEN, Wm. Hunt Smith, Wm.	Buckingham	1774	8	
ALLERMAN, John Kingston Parish	Gloucester	1774	4	
ALLERMAN, John Kingston Parish	Gloucester	1775	4	
ALLIN, James	James City	1768	1	

Name	County	Year	Tith-ables	Acres
ALLIN, Jones	James City	1768	2	250
ALMUND, Edmund	Gloucester	1770	1	
ALSUP, William	Hanover	1763		100
AMBLER, Edward	Hanover	1763		495
AMBLER, Edward	James City	1768	46	1050
AMBLER, Edward, Est.	James City	1769	49	1050
AMMONET, John	Buckingham	1774	1	
AMORY, Thomas Chambn.	Gloucester	1770	6	279
AMORY, Thomas Chambn.	Gloucester	1771	6	279
AMOS, Frank	Buckingham	1773	1	
AMOS, Francis	Buckingham	1774	2	
ANDERSON, Mrs. Anderson, Henry	Buckingham	1773	4	
ANDERSON, Ann Mrs.	Buckingham	1774	1	
ANDERSON, Edward Kingston Parish	Gloucester	1774	6	
ANDERSON, Edward Kingston Parish	Gloucester	1775	6	
ANDERSON, Bartlett	Hanover	1763	(1761)	150
ANDERSON. Benja.	Hanover	1763		150
ANDERSON, David	Hanover	1763		1244
ANDERSON, David	Stafford	1768		330
ANDERSON, David	Buckingham	1773	1	
ANDERSON, David, Exrs.	Stafford	1773	1	330
ANDERSON, Henry	Hanover	1763		201
ANDERSON, Henry, see Anderson, Mrs.				
ANDERSON, Henry	Buckingham	1774	2	
ANDERSON, James	Hanover	1763	(1756)	265
ANDERSON, James "New Kent Shfs. fee"	James City	1768		
ANDERSON, John	Hanover	1763		200
Do				100
ANDERSON, Mary	Hanover	1763		220
ANDERSON, Matthew St. Martin's Parish	Hanover	1770	5	275
ANDERSON, Matthew Junr. St. Martin's Parish	Hanover	1770	1	
ANDERSON, Matthew Kingston Parish	Gloucester	1774		
ANDERSON, Matthew	Gloucester	1775		
ANDERSON, Micajah	Buckingham	1773	1	
ANDERSON, Micajah	Buckingham	1774	1	
ANDERSON, Nathaniel	Buckingham	1773	3	
ANDERSON, Nathaniel	Buckingham	1774	3	
ANDERSON, Nelson	Hanover	1763		672
Do				100
ANDERSON, Pouncey	Hanover	1763		1114
ANDERSON, Richard	Hanover	1763		200
ANDERSON, Robert	Hanover	1763		721
Do				213
ANDERSON, Sarah	Hanover	1763		210
ANDERSON, Thomas	Hanover	1763		335
ANDERSON, William	Gloucester	1770		
ANDERSON, William	Gloucester	1770		10
ANDERSON, William	Buckingham	1773	8	
ANDERSON, William	Buckingham	1774	7	
ANDERTON, Isaac Kingston Parish	Gloucester	1774	1	
ANDERTON, Isaac Kingston Parish	Gloucester	1775	1	

Name	County	Year	Tith-ables	Acres
ANDERTON, John	Gloucester	1774	1	
Kingston Parish				
ANDERTON, John	Gloucester	1775	1	
Kingston Parish				
ANDERTON, John	Gloucester	1774	2	
Kingston Parish				
ANDERTON, John	Gloucester	1775	2	
Kingston Parish				
ANDERTON, William Senr.	Gloucester	1774		
Kingston Parish				
ANDERTON, William Senr.	Gloucester	1775		
Kingston Parish				
ANGLE, Jos., see Anglin, Adrian				
ANGLIN, Adran	Buckingham	1773	2	
Anglin, Jos.				
ANGLIN, Adrian	Buckingham	1774	2	
Angle, Jos.				
Anglin, Adrian, Junr.				
ANGLIN, Adrian, see Phelps, John				
ANGLIN, Adrian, Junr., see Anglin, Adrian				
ANGLIN, Isaac, see Anglin, William				
ANGLIN, Jos., see Anglin, Adran				
ANGLIN, Philip	Buckingham	1773	1	
ANGLIN, William	Buckingham	1773	2	
Anglin, Isaac				
ANGLIN, William	Buckingham	1774	2	
Anglin, Isaac				
ANTHONY, James	Hanover	1763		200
ANTHONY, John	Hanover	1763		400
ANTHONY, Luke	Hanover	1763		400
ARCHER, John	Hanover	1763		245
ARMISTEAD, Currel	Gloucester	1774	4	
Kingston Parish				
ARMISTEAD, Currel	Gloucester	1775	4	
Kingston Parish				
ARMISTEAD, Dorathy	Gloucester	1774	3	
Kingston Parish				
ARMISTEAD, Dorathy	Gloucester	1775	3	
Kingston Parish				
ARMISTEAD, George	Gloucester	1774	6	
Kingston Parish				
ARMISTEAD, George	Gloucester	1775	6	
Kingston Parish				
ARMISTEAD, Isaac	Gloucester	1774	1	
Kingston Parish				
ARMISTEAD, Isaac	Gloucester	1775	1	
Kingston Parish				
ARMISTEAD, John	Gloucester	1774	8	
Kingston Parish				
ARMISTEAD, John	Gloucester	1775	8	
Kingston Parish				
ARMISTEAD, Richard	Gloucester	1774	1	
Kingston Parish				
ARMISTEAD, Richard	Gloucester	1775	1	
Kingston Parish				
ARMISTEAD, Robert	Gloucester	1774	4	
Kingston Parish				
ARMISTEAD, Robert	Gloucester	1775	4	
Kingston Parish				
ARMISTEAD, Robert Junr.	Gloucester	1774	6	

Name	County	Year	Tithables	Acres
Kingston Parish ARMISTEAD, Robert Junr.	Gloucester	1775	6	
Kingston Parish ARMISTEAD, William	Gloucester	1774	11	
Kingston Parish ARMISTEAD, William	Gloucester	1775	11	
Kingston Parish ARMISTEAD, Wm.	James City	1768		
ARNOLD, Benjamin	Buckingham	1773	8	
Arnold, Edward				
ARNOLD, Benjamin	Buckingham	1774	6	
ARNOLD, Edward	Buckingham	1774	1	
ARNOLD, Edward, see Arnold, Benjamin				
ARNOLD, Joshua	Hanover	1763		148
ARRINGTON, Adler	Buckingham	1774	1	
ARRINGTON, Samuel	Buckingham	1773	1	
ASHBY, John	Stafford	1768		100
ASHBY, John	Stafford	1773		200
ASHBY, Robert	Stafford	1768		52
ASHBY, Robert Exers.	Stafford	1773		52
ASHBY, Thos., see Payne, Daniel				
ASHCROFT, Mary	James City	1768	2	217
ASHER, John, see Bolling, Robert Jr. Col.				
ASHEWORTH, Thomas	Buckingham	1774	1	
ASHLOCK, Cole	James City	1768	1	50
ASHLOCK, Cole	James City	1769	2	50
ASHLOCK, John	James City	1769	1	
ASLEY, Samuel	James City	1768	8	235
ASLEY, Samuel	James City	1769	9	235
ATKINS, Job, see Spencer, Francis West				
ATKINS, Peter	Buckingham	1773	2	
ATKINSON, Henry	Hanover	1763		210
ATKINSON, William	Hanover	1763		310
AUSTIN, Archelus	Buckingham	1773	7	
Austin, Elijah				
AUSTIN, Archelaus	Buckingham	1774	8	
Carter, Elisha				
AUSTIN, Gabriel	Gloucester	1770	1	
AUSTIN, Gabriel	Gloucester	1771	1	
AUSTIN, Thomas	James City	1768	1	
insolvent				
AUSTIN, William	Hanover	1763		340
AUSTON, John	Gloucester	1770	1	
AUSTON, John	Gloucester	1771	1	
AXLEY, James	Buckingham	1773	1	
AXLEY, James	Buckingham	1774	1	
AYLET, Philip	Hanover	1763		1000
AYRES, John, see Ayres, Matthias				
AYRES, Matthias	Buckingham	1773	5	
Ayres, John				
AYRES, Matthias	Buckingham	1774	4	
Ayres, John				
AYRES, Mathias, see Salle, William Senr.				
AYRES, Samuel	Hanover	1763	(1762)	400
AYRES, Samuel	Buckingham	1773	2	
Flood, Henry				
AYRES, Samuel	Buckingham	1774	2	
Flood, Henry				
AYRES, Nathan	Buckingham	1773	4	
AYRES, Nathan	Buckingham	1774	4	

Name	County	Year	Tithables	Acres
BABER, George, see Sanders, Thomas				
BABER, Thomas, see Scruggs, William				
BABER, Wm.	Buckingham	1773	3	
BABER, Wm.	Buckingham	1774	3	
BACON, Edmund	James City	1768		
BACON, Edmund	James City	1768		
BADGET, William	James City	1768	1	
BAGBY, John	Hanover	1763		297
BAGBY, Robt.	Buckingham	1774	3	
BAGBY, Thomas	Hanover	1763		100
BAILEY, Anselem	Hanover	1763		226
BAILEY, Ben, see Turpin, Thos.				
BAILEY, Richard	Buckingham	1773	1	
BAILEY, Richard	Buckingham	1774	1	
BAILEY, Thomas	Gloucester	1774	8	
BAILEY, Thomas Kingston Parish	Gloucester	1775	8	
BAILEY, Thomas, see Bailey, William				
BAILEY, William	Hanover	1763		250
Do.		1761	(1761)	60
BAILEY, William Bailey, Thomas	Buckingham	1773	4	
BAILEY, William Bailey, Thomas	Buckingham	1774	4	
BAILEY, Yancey, see Curd, Wm., Estate of				
BAIRD, Archibald	Buckingham	1774	1	
BAIRD, Archibald, see Baird, Henry				
BAIRD, Hardeman	Buckingham	1774	1	
BAIRD, Henry Baird, Archibald Baird, Henry Taylor, John	Buckingham	1773	4	
BAIRD, Henry	Buckingham	1774	1	
BAIRD, Henry, see Baird, Henry				
BAIRD, John	Buckingham	1773	1	
BAKER, Ambose*	Gloucester	1770		
BAKER, Benjamin*	Gloucester	1770		
BAKER, Henry Baker, Henry Jr.	Buckingham	1773	3	
BAKER, James*	Gloucester	1770		
BAKER, Jerman	James City	1768	7	
BAKER, Jerman	James City	1769	7	
BAKER, Martin	Hanover	1763		400
Do				100
Do New Patent first due 1764				104
BAKER, William Senr.*	Gloucester	1770		
BALES, Yearls, of P. Wiggenton	Stafford	1768		73
BALKINS, John, see Winstone, Anthony				
BALL, ____, see Hansbrough, Peter				
BALLON, William Cabell	Buckingham	1774	1	
BALLOW, Leonard	Buckingham	1773	1	
BALLOW, Leonard	Buckingham	1774	1	
BALLOW, Thos. Breedlove, Wm.	Buckingham	1774	4	
BANKS, Andrew	James City	1768	4	50
BANKS, Andrew	James City	1769	4	50
BANKS, Richard	James City	1768	1	
BANKS, William	James City	1768	2	35
BANKS, William	James City	1769	2	35
BARBEE, Thomas, Execr.	Stafford	1773		500

Name	County	Year	Tithables	Acres
(see Barby)				
BARBIE, George	Gloucester	1770	1	
BARBIE, George	Gloucester	1771	2	
BARBY, Thomas, Exrs.	Stafford	1768		500
(see Barbee)				
BARCLAY, George	Hanover	1770	13	1314
St. Martin's Parish				
BARHAM, Charles	James City	1768	6	550
BARHAM, Charles	James City	1769	6	550
BARHAM, Robert	James City	1768	6	148
BARHAM, Robert	James City	1769	6	148
BARKER, Charles	Hanover	1763		100
Do		1762	(1762)	100
Do				309
BARKER, Edward	Hanover	1763		50
BARKER, George	Hanover	1763		265
BARKER, John	Hanover	1763		100
BARKER, John Jun.	Hanover	1763		126
BARKER, Thomas	Hanover	1763	(1759)	150
BARKLEY, Edmund	Hanover	1763		2798
(BERKLEY)				
BARKLEY, Nelson	Hanover	1763		3000
(BERKLEY)				
BARKSDALE, Hickerson	Buckingham	1773	7	
Barksdale, John				
Dangerfield, Hawkeler				
BARKSDALE, Hickerson	Buckingham	1774	6	
BARKSDALE, Wm.	Buckingham	1773	2	
BARKSDALE, Wm.	Buckingham	1774	2	
BARNES, James	Hanover	1763	29	
BARRETT, Martha	James City	1768	4	300
BARRETT, Martha	James City	1769	6	300
BARRETT, William	James City	1768	9	300
BARRETT, William	James City	1769	10	300
BARROW, John	James City	1768		
BARTLOT, George	Hanover	1763		100
BASSET, Burwell	Hanover	1763		687
BASSET, Sarah	Gloucester	1774		
Kingston Parish				
BASSET, Sarah	Gloucester	1775		
Kingston Parish				
BASSETT, William	Gloucester	1774	1	
Kingston Parish				
BASSETT, William	Gloucester	1775	1	
BASSETT, William Junr.	Gloucester	1774	2	
Kingston Parish				
BASSETT, William Junr.	Gloucester	1775	2	
Kingston Parish				
BATES, Cannon, see Bates, John				
BATES, James	James City	1768		283
BATES, John	Buckingham	1773	9	
Bates, Cannon				
Scruggs, Wm.				
BATES, John	Buckingham	1774	6	
Stevison, James				
BATES, Thomas	Hanover	1763		65
BATES, Thomas	Gloucester	1770	1	
BATES, Thomas	Gloucester	1771	1	
BATH, Edward	Gloucester	1770	1	
BATH, Edward	Gloucester	1771	1	

Name	County	Year	Tith-ables	Acres
BATTOOE, James	Stafford	1768		100
BATTOOE, James	Stafford	1773		100
BAUGHN, Elkanch	Hanover	1763		
New Patent for 50 acres first due for 1764				
BAULDOCK, Richard, see Whitney, Jeremiah				
BAXTER, Henry	James City	1768		
BAXTER, James, see Hunter, James				
BAXTER, John	Gloucester	1774	1	
Kingston Parish				
BAXTER, John	Gloucester	1775	1	
Kingston Parish				
BAYTOP, James (Estate of)	Gloucester	1770	5	439
BAYTOP, James (Estate of)	Gloucester	1771	5	439
BAYTOP, Sarah	Gloucester	1770	9	220
BAYTOP, Sarah	Gloucester	1771	9	220
BEABER, Ambros, see Scruggs, William				
BEALK, John	Buckingham	1774	1	
BEAZLEY, John	Buckingham	1773	5	
Beazley, Jonathan				
Beasley, Wm.				
BEAZLEY, John	Buckingham	1774	6	
Beazley, Jonathan				
Beasley, Wm.				
BECKERTON, Ann*	Gloucester	1770		
BECKHAM, James	Buckingham	1774	2	
BELL, Adam Mr.	Gloucester	1770		
BELL, George	Hanover	1763		140
BELL, Henry	Buckingham	1773	6	
Spencer, Charles				
BELL, Henry	Buckingham	1774	7	
Spencer, Charles				
BELL, John	Stafford	1768		154
BELL, John	Stafford	1773		143
BELL, Judith	Buckingham	1773		
Harrison, Benja.				
BELL, Judith	Buckingham	1774	17	
BELL, More	Hanover	1763		50
BELLAMY, William	Gloucester	1770	4	60
BELLAMY, William	Gloucester	1771	4	60
BELSHES, Patrick	Hanover	1763		851
BELSCHES, Judith decd	Hanover	1770		763(?)
(St. Martin's)				
BELVIN, John	Gloucester	1770	1	
BELVIN, John	Gloucester	1771	1	
BELVIN, Lewis	Gloucester	1770	1	
BELVIN, Lewis	Gloucester	1771	1	
BELVIN, William	Gloucester	1771	1	
BELWIN, Henry (BELVIN)	Gloucester	1770	2	
BELWIN, Henry (BELVIN)	Gloucester	1771	2	
BENNET, Henry*	Gloucester	1770		
BENNING, James	Buckingham	1773	6	
BENNING, John	Buckingham	1773	9	
Worley, John				
BENNING, Jno.	Buckingham	1774	10	
Bondurant, Joel				
Worley, John, Miller				
BENNING, Joseph Capt.	Buckingham	1773	6	
BENNING, Joseph	Buckingham	1774	5	

Name	County	Year	Tithables	Acres
Hicks, Hickerson				
BENTLEY, James*	Gloucester	1770	5	
BENTLEY, James*	Gloucester	1771	5	
BERKLEY, Edmund	Gloucester	1770		450
BERNARD, John	Buckingham	1773	10	
Pryer, John				
BERNARD, John Junr.	Buckingham	1773	1	
BERNARD, John Senr.	Buckingham	1774	11	
Bernard, John Junr.				
Bernard, Robert				
Smith, Robt.				
BERNARD, Robert	Buckingham	1773	1	
BERRYMAN, Christopher	Hanover	1763		385
BERRYMAN, Isaac	Buckingham	1773	5	
Berryman, Christopher				
BERRYMAN, Isaac	Buckingham	1774	5	
Berryman, Christopher, son				
BERRYMAN, Isaac	Buckingham	1774	2	
Berryman, Wm., son				
BERRYMAN, John	Stafford	1768		298
BERRYMAN, John, Exr.	Stafford	1768		1310
of Gibson and Benjamin				
BERRYMAN, John, Exr.	Stafford	1773		1012
of Gibson and Benjamin				
"belongs to somebody in Fairfax"				
BERRYMAN, Wm., son, see Berryman, Isaac				
BERSKERVALL, John	Buckingham	1774	1	
BESKERVALL, Geo.	Buckingham	1774	1	
BEVERIDGE, John	Gloucester	1770	4	
BEW, William	Gloucester	1770	1	
BICKERTON, John	Hanover	1763		600
"Land afterwards purch'd by S.G."				
BICKLEY, Wm.	Hanover	1770	3	
St. Martin's Parish				
BILLUPS, Humphrey	Gloucester	1774	3	
Kingston Parish				
BILLUPS, Humphrey	Gloucester	1775	3	
Kingston Parish				
BILLUPS, John Junr.*	Gloucester	1770		
and William				
BILLUPS, John Senr.	Gloucester	1774	15	
Kingston Parish				
BILLUPS, John Senr.	Gloucester	1775	15	
Kingston Parish				
BILLUPS, Joseph, Estate	Gloucester	1774	7	
Kingston Parish				
BILLUPS, Joseph, Estate	Gloucester	1775	7	
Kingston Parish				
BILLUPS, Robert	Gloucester	1774	37	
Kingston Parish				
BILLUPS, Robert	Gloucester	1775	37	
Kingston Parish				
BILLUPS, Robert Junr.	Gloucester	1774	6	
Kingston Parish				
BILLUPS, Robert Junr.	Gloucester	1775	6	
Kingston Parish				
BILLUPS, Thomas	Gloucester	1774	9	
Kingston Parish				
BILLUPS, Thomas	Gloucester	1775	9	
Kingston Parish				

Name	County	Year	Tith-ables	Acres
BILLUPS, William, see Billups, John Junr.				
BINGHAM, Josias	Hanover	1763		100
BINGHAM, Josias, Jun.	Hanover	1763		100
BINGHAM, Stephen	James City	1768	3	1400
BINGHAM, Stephen	James City	1769	3	1400
BINGLEY, Nathaniel	James City	1768	6	60
BINGLEY, Nathaniel	James City	1769	7	60
BINION, Martin	Buckingham	1774	1	
BINION, William	Buckingham	1773	6	
BINION, Wm.	Buckingham	1774	6	
BINNS, John	Buckingham	1774		
BIRKS, Charles	Buckingham	1773	2	
BIRKS, Charles	Buckingham	1774	2	
BIRKS, John	Buckingham	1773	2	
BIRKS, John	Buckingham	1774	2	
BISHOP, Wm., see Howard Benja. Majr. Estate		1773		
BLACK, Elenore	Hanover	1763		80
BLACKBURN, Jacob, see Blackburn Lambeth Tye				
BLACKBURN, Jacob, see Blackburn, Lambuth				
BLACKBURN, John	Buckingham	1774	1	
BLACKBURN, John, see Maloid, David				
BLACKBURN, Lambuth	Buckingham	1773	4	
Blackburn, Jacob				
Blackburn, Thomas				
BLACKBURN, Lambeth Tye	Buckingham	1774	3	
Blackburn, Jacob				
BLACKBURN, Thomas	Buckingham	1774	1	
BLACKBURN, Thomas, see Blackburn, Lambuth				
BLACKLEY, George	Gloucester	1770		
BLACKLEY, George	Gloucester	1771		
BLACKLEY, John	Gloucester	1770		
BLACKWELL, John Jun.	Hanover	1763		220
BLACKWELL, John	Hanover	1763		100
BLACKWELL, Josias	Hanover	1763		342
BLACKWELL, Micajah	Hanover	1763		800
Do		1762	(1762)	100
BLAIR, John Jr., Mr.	James City	1768		
BLAIR, John Esqr.	Hanover	1763		1750
Do				915
BLAIR, John Esqr. "also 4 county thithes, 235 acres"	James City	1768	18	1953
BLAIR, John Esqr.	James City	1769	18	1953
BLAKE, Thomas Kingston Parish	Gloucester	1774	4	
BLAKE, Thomas Kingston Parish	Gloucester	1775	4	
BLAKEY, Robert	Buckingham	1773	2	
BLAKEY, Thomas Blakey, Thomas Jr.	Buckingham	1773	11	
BLAKEY, Thomas Blakey, Thomas Jr. Blakey, Wm. Edens, Alexr.	Buckingham	1774	12	
BLALOCK, Kade	Hanover	1763		123
BLALOCK, Sarah	Hanover	1763	(1756)	123

Name	County	Year	Tithables	Acres
BLAND, Francis	Gloucester	1770	1	
BLAND, Francis	Gloucester	1771	1	
BLAND, Wm., Rev.	James City	1769	6	
BLANKS, Richard	Buckingham	1773	5	
BLANKS, Richard	Buckingham	1774	7	
BLASSINGHAM, James	Gloucester	1770	3	
BLASSINGHAM, James	Gloucester	1771	2	
BLASSINGHAM, John*	Gloucester	1770		
BLASSINGANE, John, see Massey, Robert				
BLASSINGHAM, Sarah	Gloucester	1770	1	
BLASSINGHAM, Sarah	Gloucester	1771	1	
BLASSINGHAM, William (wife's land)	Gloucester	1770	1	
BLASSINGHAM, William (wife's land)	Gloucester	1771	1	
BLISSLAND PARISH	James City	1768		
BLUNT, Barthw.*	Gloucester	1770		
BLUNT, Page	Hanover	1763		580
do				200
BOATWRIGHT, James	Hanover	1763		240
BOATWRIGHT, Jesse	Buckingham	1774	1	
BOAZ, Archibald	Buckingham	1773	1	
BOAZ, Daniel	Buckingham	1773	1	
BOAZ, Daniel	Buckingham	1774	1	
BOAZ, Mesheck, see Boaz, Thomas				
BOAZ, Thomas Boaz, Mesheck	Buckingham	1773	2	
BOAZ, Thomas	Buckingham	1774	2	
BOAZE, Robt., see King, Walter				
BOCOCK, John	Buckingham	1773	1	
BOGLE, Robt.	James City	1768		
BOHANNON, William Kingston Parish	Gloucester	1774	3	
BOHANNON, William Kingston Parish	Gloucester	1775	3	
BOLLING, Archibald	Buckingham	1773	7	
BOLLING, Archibald Woodson, Anderson	Buckingham	1773	7	
BOLLING, Archibald Garrett, John McLoud, John	Buckingham	1774	11	
BOLLING, Robert, Col.	Buckingham	1773	20	
BOLLING, Robert Jr. Col. Shaw, William Roy, Peter Asher, John Cooper, Jacob	Buckingham	1774	24	
BONDURANT, Darby	Buckingham	1773	1	
BONDURANT, David	Buckingham	1773	1	
BONDURANT, Joel, see Benning, Jno.				
BONDURANT, John Junr.	Buckingham	1773	1	
BOLTON, Mary Kingston Parish	Gloucester	1774		
BOLTON, Mary Kingston Parish	Gloucester	1775		
BOOKER, Lewis	Gloucester	1770	15	500
BOOKER, Lewis	Gloucester	1771	15	500
BOOKER, Mary	Gloucester	1770	11	490
BOOKER, Mary	Gloucester	1771	10	490

Name	County	Year	Tithables	Acres
Booker, Richard	Gloucester	1770		
BOOTHE, Boaze	James City	1769	2	
BOOTH, George	Gloucester	1770	19	501
BOOTH, George	Gloucester	1771	20	501
BOOTH, George Junr.	Gloucester	1770	43	1150
BOOTH, George Junr.	Gloucester	1771	45	1150
BOOTH, Thomas	Gloucester	1770	15	350
BOOTH, Thos., see Steward, James				
BOOTWRIGHT, James, see Cabell, Joseph Col.				
BOOTWRIGHT, Jesse, see Nicholas, John				
BORUM, Benjamin	Hanover	1763		100
BORUM, Edmund Kingston Parish	Gloucester	1774	5	
BORUM, Edmund Kingston Parish	Gloucester	1775	5	
BORUM, Edmund Senr. Kingston Parish	Gloucester	1774	6	
BORUM, Edmund Senr. Kingston Parish	Gloucester	1775	6	
BORUM, William Kingston Parish	Gloucester	1774	1	
BORUM, William Kingston Parish	Gloucester	1775	1	
BOSE, Daniel	Hanover	1763		99
BOSS, John Kingston Parish	Gloucester	1774	1	
BOSS, John Kingston Parish	Gloucester	1775	1	
BOSTICK, John	Buckingham	1773	4	
BOSTICK, John Rosberry, Wm.	Buckingham	1774	4	
BOSWELL, Elizabeth	Gloucester	1770	5	73
BOSWELL, Elizabeth	Gloucester	1771	7	73
BOSWELL, George "to Clerk's note from K. Wm. for Est."	Gloucester	1770		232
BOSWELL, James*	Gloucester	1770		
BOSWELL, James*	Gloucester	1771		
BOSWELL, John	Gloucester	1770	3	
BOSWELL, John	Gloucester	1771		
BOSWELL, John shoe makr.	Gloucester	1770	2	
BOSWELL, John	Gloucester	1771	1	
BOSWELL, John	Hanover	1763		319
BOSWELL, Thomas	Hanover	1763		337
BOSWELL, Thomas	Gloucester	1770	13	728
BOSWELL, Thomas	Gloucester	1771	11	728
BOSWELL, William (Brunswick)*	Gloucester	1770		
BOTTS, Seth	Stafford	1768		852
BOTTS, Seth	Stafford	1773		852
do of Leeright, P. Wm.				180
BOUNCHER, Nehemiah	Hanover	1763	(1761)	50
BOURN, Sarah	Hanover	1763		60
BOWCOCK, Edward James Southall's Exr.	James City	1768		
BOWE, Henry	Hanover	1763		200
BOWE, Nathaniel	Hanover	1763		434
BOWLES, Benjamin	Hanover	1763		633
BOWLES, David	Buckingham	1774	1	

Name	County	Year	Tithables	Acres
BOWLES, Deborah	Hanover	1763		300
BOWLES, Elizabeth	Hanover	1763		412
BOWLES, Isaac	James City	1768	3	
BOWLES, Isaac	James City	1769	3	
BOWLES, John Middlesex	Hanover	1763		200
BOWLES, Mary	Hanover	1763		200
Do				350
BOWLES, Thomas	Hanover	1763		510
BOWLES, Thomas Jun.	Hanover	1763		300
BOWLES, William	James City	1769	1	
BOWRY, John	James City	1768		
BOYD, James	Hanover	1763		360
BOYLE, Wm., see Winstone, Anthony				
BRADLEY, John	James City	1769	2	
BRADLEY, John, see Curd, Joseph				
BRADLEY, William	Hanover	1763		200
BRADLY, Wm.	Buckingham	1773	1	
BRADLY, Wm.	Buckingham	1774	2	
BRADLEY, Wm.	Buckingham	1774	3	
Garthard, John B.				
BRADY, Jos.	Buckingham	1773	1	
BRAIN, Robert	Hanover	1763		200
BRAMMER, James	Buckingham	1773	1	
BRAMMER, John	Buckingham	1773	1	
BRAMMER, John, Junr.	Buckingham	1773		
Manning, Davis				
BRAMMER, John Jur.	Buckingham	1774	1	
BRAY, George (Est. of)	Gloucester	1770	3	
BRAY, George (Est. of)	Gloucester	1771		
BREEDLOVE, Mary	Gloucester	1770		
BREEDLOVE, Mary	Gloucester	1771		
BREEDLOVE, Wm., see Ballow, Thos.				
BRENT, George	Stafford	1768		2300
BRENT, George	Stafford	1773		1700
BRENT, Robert	Stafford	1768		470
BRENT, Robert	Stafford	1773		470
"140 Acres sold to Alexr. Gaddess & C."				
BRENT, William	Stafford	1768		6952
BRENT, William	Stafford	1773		6952
BRENT, William Maryland	Stafford	1768		1400
BRENT, William Maryland	Stafford	1773		1400
BREWER, Sackvile	James City	1768		
BRIDWELL, Abraham	Stafford	1768		718
BRIDEWELL, Abraham Jr.	Stafford	1773		133
BRIDEWELL, Abraham	Stafford	1773		200
"100 A. to John Bridewell"				
"100 A. to Withers King"				
BRIDWELL, Isaac	Stafford	1768		102
BRIDWELL, Isaac	Stafford	1773		102
BRIDWELL, Isaac, see King, Elisabeth				
BRIDWELL, John	Stafford	1768		220
BRIDWELL, John	Stafford	1773		220
BRIDEWELL, John, see Bridewell, Abraham				
BRIDWELL, Moses	Stafford	1768		133
BRIDWELL, Moses	Stafford	1773		133
BRIDWELL, Samuel	Stafford	1768		134
BRIDWELL, Samuel	Stafford	1773		134
BRIDWELL, William	Stafford	1768		130
BRIDEWELL, William	Stafford	1773		133
BRIDGE, William	Gloucester	1774	1	

Name	County	Year	Tithables	Acres
Kingston Parish				
BRIDGE, William	Gloucester	1775	1	
Kingston Parish				
BRIDGES, George	James City	1768	4	208
BRIDGES, George	James City	1769	4	208
BRIDGES, John	Gloucester	1770		
BRIDGES, John	Gloucester	1771		
BRIGGS, James*	Gloucester	1770		
BRISTOW, James	Buckingham	1773	10	
BRISTOW, James	Buckingham	1774	8	
Martin, George				
BRISTOW, Robert	Gloucester	1770	36	2000
BRISTOW, Robert	Gloucester	1771	37	2000
BRISTOW, Robert Estate	Gloucester	1774	12	
Kingston Parish				
BRISTOW, Robert Estate	Gloucester	1775	12	
Kingston Parish				
BRISTOW, Thompson, see Saunders, Robt.				
BROADRIB's Esta.	James City	1768		177
BROCKS, Richard	Stafford	1773		180
BRONAUGH, John of Jno. Carter	Stafford	1768		307
BRONAUGH, John	Stafford	1773		370
BROOK(S), Thomas, see Walker, James				
BROOKES, George	Gloucester	1774	3	
Kingston Parish				
BROOKES, George	Gloucester	1775	3	
BROOKS, Richard	Stafford	1768		180
BROOKS, Thomas	Hanover	1763		40
BROOKS, Thomas, see Walker, James				
BROOKING, Samuel*	Gloucester	1770		
BROTHERS, John	Buckingham	1773	2	
BROTHERS, John	Buckingham	1774	2	
BROWN, Allen, see Brown, John				
BROWN, Allen Senr.	Buckingham	1774	1	
BROWN, Ann	Gloucester	1770		
BROWN, Benjamin	Hanover	1763		167
Do				716
BROWN, Charles	Gloucester	1770	1	
BROWN, Charles	Gloucester	1771	1	
BROWN, Charles Junr.	Gloucester	1771	1	
BROWN, Dudley	Hanover	1770	2	
St. Martin's Parish				
BROWN, Edmund	Hanover	1763		300
BROWN, Francis, Kingston Parish	Gloucester	1774	2	
BROWN, Francis, Kingston Parish	Gloucester	1775	2	
BROWN, George, Kingston Parish	Gloucester	1774	6	
BROWN, George, Kingston Parish	Gloucester	1775	6	
BROWN, Henry	James City	1768	7	
BROWN, Henry	James City	1769	7	
BROWN, I(s)hum	Buckingham	1774	2	
Brown, Wilson				
BROWN, James	Buckingham	1773	2	
Brown, James Nevill				
BROWN, James	Buckingham	1774	1	
BROWN, John	Hanover	1763		165
BROWN, John	Buckingham	1773	2	
Brown, Allen				
BROWN, John	James City	1768	2	50
BROWN, John	James City	1768	2	
BROWN, John	James City	1769	3	

Name	County	Year	Tithables	Acres
BROWN, John, Estate	James City	1769	2	50
BROWN, John, Jr.	Buckingham	1773	1	
BROWN, John, Jr.	Buckingham	1774	1	
BROWN, John Senr.	Buckingham	1774	1	
BROWN, John "(son John Senr.)"	Buckingham	1774	1	
BROWN, John (Taylor)	Gloucester	1770	1	
BROWN, Joseph	Gloucester	1771	1	
BROWN, Joseph	Buckingham	1774	1	
BROWN, Mary	James City	1768	11	1150
BROWN, Mary	James City	1769	11	1150
BROWN, Matthew	Hanover	1763		175
BROWN, Richard May(s)	Stafford	1773		155
BROWN, Richd. Revd. In Maryland	Stafford	1768		155
BROWN, Robert	Hanover	1763		100
BROWN, Sheldrake	Hanover	1763		409
BROWN, Thomas	Gloucester	1770	1	
BROWN, Thomas	Gloucester	1771	1	
BROWN, Wilson, see Brown, I(s)hum				
BROWN, William	Hanover	1763		150
Do				100
Do				100
BROWN, William	James City	1768	11	552
BROWN, William	James City	1768	3	
BROWN, William	James City	1769	3	
BROWN, William	James City	1769	11	318
BROWN, William, Kingston Parish	Gloucester	1774	1	
BROWN, William, Kingston Parish	Gloucester	1775	1	
BROWN, William Jur.	James City	1768	4	
BROWN, William Jur.	James City	1769	3	
BROWNE, John	Buckingham	1774	1	
BROWNING, John	Hanover	1763		125
BROWNLEY, Archibald Kingston Parish	Gloucester	1774	2	
BROWNLEY, Archibald Kingston Parish	Gloucester	1775	2	
BROWNLEY, Archibald Junr. Kingston Parish	Gloucester	1774	1	
BROWNLEY, Archibald Junr. Kingston Parish	Gloucester	1775	1	
BROWNLEY, Edward (Kingston Parish)	Gloucester	1774	1	
BROWNLEY, Edward (Kingston Parish)	Gloucester	1775	1	
BROWNLEY, Elizabeth Kingston Parish	Gloucester	1774		
BROWNLEY, Elizabeth Kingston Parish	Gloucester	1775		
BROWNLEY, James (Kingston Parish)	Gloucester	1774	2	
BROWNLEY, James (Kingston Parish)	Gloucester	1775	2	
BROWNLEY, William Senr. Kingston Parish	Gloucester	1774	1	
BROWNLEY, William Senr. Kingston Parish	Gloucester	1775	1	
BRUCE, Jacob	James City	1768	4	100
BRUCE, Jacob	James City	1769	3	100
BRYAN, Ben	James City	1768		
BRYAN, Benjamin	James City	1768		
BRYAN, Frederick	James City	1769		
BRYANT, Isaac	Buckingham	1773	2	
BRYANT, Isaac	Buckingham	1774	3	
BRYANT, John	Buckingham	1774	2	
BRYANT, William	Buckingham	1773	1	

Name	County	Year	Tithables	Acres
BUCKHENNON, John	Gloucester	1771	1	
BUCKNER, Baldwin	Gloucester	1770	25	800
BUCKNER, Baldwin	Gloucester	1771	22	800
BUCKNER, Baldwin, see Chapman, Henry				
BUCKNER, John	Gloucester	1770	3	
BUCKNER, John	Gloucester	1771	3	
BUCKNER, John Junr.	Gloucester	1770	9	200
BUCKNER, John Junr.	Gloucester	1771	10	200
BUCKNER, Mary	Gloucester	1770		
pd. by John Buckner				
BUCKNER, Mary	Gloucester	1771		
pd. by John Buckner				
BUCKNER, William	Gloucester	1774	5	
Kingston Parish				
BUCKNER, William	Gloucester	1775	5	
Kingston Parish				
BUFFIN, John	James City	1768	3	110
BUFORD, Milton	Buckingham	1773	1	
BUFORD, Thomas	Buckingham	1773	1	
BULLOCK, Edward	Hanover	1763		300
BULLOCK, Paterson	Hanover	1763		390
BULLOCK, Richd.	Hanover	1763	(1757)	254
BUMPASS, Samuel	Hanover	1763		839
BUMPASS, William	Buckingham	1773	1	
BUNBURY, Elis, see Bunbury, Thomas Junr.				
BUNBURY, Elisabeth	Stafford	1773		749
BUNBURY, Thomas Jr.	Stafford	1768		162
BUNBURY, Thomas Junr.	Stafford	1773		912
"148 acres sold to Elis.(?) Bunbury"				
BUNBURY, Thomas Senr.	Stafford	1768		150
BUNBURY, Thomas Senr.	Stafford	1773		150
BUNBURRY, Thos., see Whiting, John				
BUNBURY, William, Exors.	Stafford	1768		1499
BUNDERANT, Joel	Buckingham	1773	1	
BUNDURANT, Darby	Buckingham	1774	1	
BUNDURANT, John	Buckingham	1774	1	
BUNDURANT, John Jur.	Buckingham	1774	1	
BUNDURANT, John Senr.	Buckingham	1773	1	
BUNDURANT, Joseph	Buckingham	1774	3	
Bundurant, Joseph Jur.				
BUNDURANT, Richard	Buckingham	1773	1	
BUNDURANT, Richard	Buckingham	1774	1	
BUNDURANT, Thomas	Buckingham	1773	3	
BURBIDG, Julius K.	James City	1768		
BURGES, Margrett	Stafford	1768		100
BURGES, Margrett	Stafford	1773		100
BURGESS, _____, see Hansbrough, Peter				
BURK, George (Tillotson Parish)	Buckingham	1773	5	
Wright, Thomas				
BURKE, Jeremiah	Gloucester	1770	1	
BURKE, Jeremiah	Gloucester	1771	2	
BURNET, Griffen, see Saunders, Samuel				
BURNET, Isaac	Hanover	1763		128
BUSH, Martha	James City	1768		50
BUSH, Thomas	James City	1768	2	40
BUSH, Thomas	James City	1769	2	40
BUSHROD, Mrs., see Whiting, John				
BUSHROD'S LAND, see Whiting, John				
BUTLER, Samuel	Hanover	1763		100
BUTLER, Susanna	Hanover	1763		300

Name	County	Year	Tithables	Acres
BUTTLER, Christopher	Hanover	1763		100
BUXTON, George, see Buxton, Wm.				
BUXTON, George, see Woodson, Jacob				
BUXTON, Jacob, see Phelps, John				
BUXTON, Wm.	Buckingham	1773	5	
Buxton, George				
BUXSTON, Wm.	Buckingham	1774	4	
BYAS or BYARS	Hanover	1763		315
Do				75
BYERS, Docr.	James City	1768		
BYNION, Martain	Buckingham	1773	1	
BYRAM, Henry, see Gannaway, Wm.				
BYRAM, Peter	Stafford	1768		250
BYRAM, William, see Cary, Archibald Col.				
BYRAN, Jane	James City	1768	2	
BYRD, William Esq.	James City	1769	8	685
CABELL, John (Tillotson Par.)	Buckingham	1773	8	
CABELL, John Colo.	Buckingham	1774	8	
Hill, Isaac				
CABELL, Joseph Col.	Buckingham	1773	17	
Bootwright, James				
Johnson, William - Overs'r				
CABELL, Joseph Colo.	Buckingham	1774		
Reynolds, David - Overseer				
Johnson, Wm. - Overseer				
CABELL, William, see Thomas, John				
CAFFEY, Robert W.	Gloucester	1770		
CAKE, Anthony	Gloucester	1770	1	
CAKE, Anthony	Gloucester	1771	1	
CALL, Richard	Gloucester	1770	3	
CALL, Richard	Gloucester	1771	3	
CALLAWN, William	Gloucester	1770		260
CALLAWN, William	Gloucester	1771	3	260
CALLIS, Ambrose, Kingston Parish	Gloucester	1774	2	
CALLIS, Ambrose, Kingston Parish	Gloucester	1775	2	
CALLIS, John, Kingston Parish	Gloucester	1774	4	
CALLIS, John, Kingston Parish	Gloucester	1775	4	
CALLIS, John Junr.	Gloucester	1774	12	
Kingston Parish				
CALLIS, John Junr.	Gloucester	1775	12	
Kingston Parish				
CALLIS, Robert, Kingston Parish	Gloucester	1774	1	
CALLIS, Robert, Kingston Parish	Gloucester	1775	1	
CAMERON, Daniel	Hanover	1763		50
CAMERON, John	Hanover	1763		75
CAMP, John	James City	1768	10	910
"4 Tithes in Blisland Parish"				
CAMP, John	James City	1769	5	310
CAMP, John	Gloucester	1770		
CAMP, John	Gloucester	1771	2	
CAMP, Thomas Junr.	Gloucester	1770	2	132
CAMP, Thomas Junr.	Gloucester	1771	8	132
CAMP, Thomas Senr.	Gloucester	1770	1	
CAMPBELL, Danl., see Nicholas, John				
CAMPBELL, Patrick, see Nicholas, John				
CANIDAY, William	Buckingham	1773	1	
CANEDAY, William	Buckingham	1774	1	
CANNADAY, Joseph	James City	1768	2	

Name	County	Year	Tithables	Acres
CANNADAY, Joseph	James City	1769	2	
CANNON, John	Buckingham	1773	12	
Davis, Joel				
Gooldsby, Charles				
CANNON, John	Buckingham	1774	9	
CANNON, William	Buckingham	1773	17	
Meggs, Joel				
CANNON, Wm.	Buckingham	1774	13	
Stanard, James				
CARDWELL, Lewis	James City	1769	2	
CARDWELL, William	James City	1769	3	
CARNER, John	Buckingham	1773	1	
CARNER, John	Buckingham	1774	1	
CARNER, William	Buckingham	1773	2	
Carner, John				
CARNER, Wm.	Buckingham	1774	2	
Carner, John, son				
CARNEY, John	Stafford	1768		180
CARNEY, Joshua	Stafford	1773		40
CARR, John Jun.	Hanover	1763		150
CARR, John, St. Martin's Parish	Hanover	1770	13	1000
CARR, Samuel	Hanover	1770	5	
St. Martin's Parish				
CARROLL, William	Gloucester	1770		
CARTER, Bailey, see Walker, Asop				
CARTER, Elisha, see Austin, Archelaus				
CARTER, George	Buckingham	1773	2	
CARTER, George	Buckingham	1774	1	
CARTER, Huddleston, see Carter, John				
CARTER, James	James City	1768	6	4
Do			10	600
CARTER, James (Prince Edward)	Gloucester	1770		
CARTER, James (Prince Edward)	Gloucester	1771		
CARTER, James Doctr.	James City	1769	8	604
"to 24 Tithes in the Pint (Point)"				
CARTER, Jas., see Carter, John				
CARTER, Jane (Kingston Parish)	Gloucester	1774	16	
CARTER, Jane (Kingston Parish)	Gloucester	1775	16	
CARTER, Jno., see Bronaugh, John				
CARTER, John	Hanover	1763		134
CARTER, John of Jas. Carter	Stafford	1768		536
CARTER, John	James City	1768	3	
CARTER, John	Stafford	1773	11	436
CARTER, John	Buckingham	1774	2	
Carter, Huddleston				
CARTER, John Esqr.	Hanover	1763		1500
CARTER, John, Mercht.	James City	1768		
CARTER, John H.	James City	1769	2	
CARTER, Joseph	Stafford	1768		500
CARTER, Joseph	Buckingham	1773	2	
CARTER, Joseph	Stafford	1773		500
CARTER, Joseph	Buckingham	1774	1	
CARTER, Lucey	Stafford	1773		100
CARTER, Robert	Hanover	1763		286
CARTER, Stephen	Buckingham	1773	1	
CARTER, Stephen	Buckingham	1774	1	
CARY, Ann (Kingston Parish)	Gloucester	1774	8	
CARY, Ann (Kingston Parish)	Gloucester	1775	8	
CARY, Archibald Col	Buckingham	1773	35	
Nelson, John				

Name	County	Year	Tithables	Acres
Byram, William				
Garrott, Henry				
Edwards, Jesse (miller)				
CARY, Archibald Col.	Buckingham	1774	21	
Nelson, John				
Byram, William				
Edwards, Jesse				
Garrott, Henry				
Sanguila, Daniel				
CARY, Dorothy (Kingston Parish)	Gloucester	1774	15	
CARY, Dorothy (Kingston Parish)	Gloucester	1775	15	
CARY, Robert	Buckingham	1773	15	
Walker, Asaph				
CARY, Robert	Buckingham	1774	13	
Walker, Asaph, overs'r				
CARY, Wilson	Gloucester	1770	37	2419
CARY, Wilson	Gloucester	1771	37	2419
CASON, Seth	Buckingham	1773	3	
Cason, Edward				
CASON, Seth	Buckingham	1774	3	
Cason, Edward				
CASON, Thomas, of Jas. Kenney	Stafford	1768		287
CASSON, Thomas	Stafford	1773		287
CASTLEN, Andrew	Hanover	1763		75
Do				107
CATHORN, John	Hanover	1763		150
CAUTHORN, James	Hanover	1763		100
CHAMBERLANE, Capt. Richd.	Buckingham	1773	29	
Morris, Benja.				
CHAMBERLANE, Capt. Richd.	Buckingham	1774	29	
CHAMBERS, Edmond, see Chambers, John Snr.				
CHAMBERS, George	Buckingham	1773	4	
CHAMBERS, John	Buckingham	1773	4	
CHAMBERS, John	Buckingham	1774	7	
Chambers, Jno. Jr.				
CHAMBERS, John Ser	Buckingham	1774	8	
Chambers, John Jnr.				
Chambers, Edmond				
CHAMBERS, Joseph	Buckingham	1774	1	
CHAMBERS, Mary (Kingston Parish)	Gloucester	1774	1	
CHAMBERS, Mary (Kingston Parish)	Gloucester	1775	1	
CHAMBERS, Wm.	Buckingham	1773	7	
CHAMBERS, Wm.	Buckingham	1774	7	
CHANCEY, Wm. Mr.	James City	1768		
CHANDLER, Abram.	Buckingham	1774	1	
CHANDLER, Richard	Hanover	1763		191
CHAPMAN, Henry	Gloucester	1770		
"costs to Baldwin Buckner's Execs."				
CHAPMAN, Nathaniel	Stafford	1768		3058
CHAPMAN, Taylor, Exrs.	Stafford	1768		
CHAPMAN, Taylor, Exrs.	Stafford	1773		
CHAPPLE, Edward	Hanover	1763		70
CHARLES, John	James City	1768		
CHARLES, Thomas	Hanover	1763		186
Do				130
CHARLTON, Edward	James City	1768		
CHARLTON, Jacob	James City	1769	1	
CHARLTON, Joseph	James City	1768	1	72
CHARLTON, Joseph	James City	1769	1	72
CHASTAIN, Abraham, see Chastain, Peter				

Name	County	Year	Tithables	Acres
CHASTAIN, A-O Beraham	Buckingham	1774	1	
CHASTAIN, Archer	Buckingham	1774	1	
CHASTAIN, Isaac	Buckingham	1773	2	
CHASTAIN, John	Buckingham	1773	1	
CHASTAIN, Peter	Buckingham	1773	2	
Chastain, Abraham				
CHASTAIN, Rane	Buckingham	1773	4	
CHASTAIN, Rane	Buckingham	1774	4	
CHASTAIN, Rene	Buckingham	1773	1	
CHASTAIN, Rene, Jr. (Rane also)	Buckingham	1773	2	
CHASTAIN, Rene, Jr.	Buckingham	1774	2	
CHILDRESS, Francis	Buckingham	1773	2	
CHILDRESS, Francis	Buckingham	1774	1	
CHILDRESS, Jno.	Buckingham	1773	2	
CHILDRESS, John	Buckingham	1774	2	
Stinson, Alexr.				
CHILDRESS, Willi__ (mutilated)	Buckingham	1773	1	
CHILDRESS, Willis	Buckingham	1774	1	
CHILDRESS, William	Hanover	1763		88
CHILDS, see Gist, Samuel				
CHISMAN, Henry	James City	1768	7	125
CHISMAN, Henry	James City	1769	7	125
CHISOLM, Mary	Hanover	1763		450
CHISWELL, Elisabeth	James City	1768	8	200
CHISELL, Elisabeth	James City	1769	9	200
CHITWOOD, John, see Cox, Matthew				
CHOWNING, Josiah	James City	1768	3	
CHOWNING, Josiah	James City	1768	4	
CHOWNING, Josiah	James City	1769	1	235
CHRISTIAN, Andrew	Hanover	1763		249
Do				150
CHRISTIAN, Archer	Buckingham	1773	1	
CHRISTIAN, Archer	Buckingham	1774	1	
CHRISTIAN, John	James City	1768		
CHRISTIAN, Lewis	Buckingham	1774	1	
CHRISTIAN, Martha	Gloucester	1774		
Kingston Parish				
CHRISTIAN, Martha	Gloucester	1775		
Kingston Parish				
CHRISTMAS, Thomas	Hanover	1763		791
CLAIBORNE, Philip Whitchead	Hanover	1763		400
CLARK, Francis	Hanover	1763		100
Do		1762	(1762)	152
CLARK, George, see Curd, Joseph				
CLARK, Isaac	Hanover	1763		100
CLARK, James	Gloucester	1770	1	149
CLARK, James	Gloucester	1771	1	149
CLARK, Rachel	Hanover	1763		170
CLAYBURN, Herbert	James City	1768		
CLAYBURN, Phillip W.	James City	1768		
CLAYBROOK, Anne	Hanover	1763		344
CLAYTON, George	Hanover	1763		133
CLAYTON, Jasper	Gloucester	1770	17	
CLAYTON, Jasper	Gloucester	1771	2	
Exec. John Read				300
CLAYTON, Jasper	Gloucester	1774		
Kingston Parish				
CLAYTON, Jasper	Gloucester	1775		
Kingston Parish				
CLAYTON, John	Gloucester	1770	19	450

Name	County	Year	Tithables	Acres
CLAYTON, John	Gloucester	1771	19	
CLAYTON, John Esqr.	Hanover	1763		266
Do				170
CLAYTON, Thomas	Gloucester	1770	16	
CLAYTON, Thomas	Gloucester	1771	9	
CLEAVER, James	Gloucester	1770	3	65
CLEAVER, John	Gloucester	1770		
CLIFT, William	Hanover	1770	2	600
St. Martin's Parish				
CLIFTON, Burdit, Exrs	Stafford	1768		306
CLIFTON, Burdit, Exrs	Stafford	1773		306
CLOAR, John	Buckingham	1774	1	
"at Moses Goings"				
CLOPTON, George	Hanover	1763		303
CLOPTON, William	Hanover	1763		110
CLOUGH, George	Hanover	1763		400
CLUVERIUS, Benjn.	Gloucester	1770	24	560
CLUVERIUS, Benjn.	Gloucester	1771	22	560
COBB, John (Tillotson Parish)	Buckingham	1773	2	
Vines, Waddy				
COBB, River Tom	Buckingham	1774	4	
COBBETTS, Henry	James City	1768	3	
COBBS, David, see Cobbs, Judith				
COBBS, Jesse, see Douglass, James				
COBBS, John	Buckingham	1774	8	
Kidd, Lewis, overseer				
COBBS, Judith & David	Hanover	1763		148
Do				145
COBBS, Thomas (at Walton's Fork)	Buckingham	1773	7	
Coupland, Henry				
COBBS, Thomas, see Howard, Benja. Majr. Estate				
COBBS, Thos.	Buckingham	1774	15	
Mayo, Thos.				
COCHRON, Messrs. & Co.	James City	1768		
COCKE, ___ Col., see West, William				
COCKE, Bowler	Hanover	1763		600
COCKE, Bowler Jun.	Hanover	1763		3210
COCKE, Bradley	Hanover	1763		165
COCK, Elisbeth	Stafford	1773		2324
COCKE, George, purchased by	Hanover	1763		350
S.G. & Measd (measured) as 377 Acres				
COCKE, Hartwell Col. Estate	Buckingham	1773	10	
Oglesby, Shadrack				
COCKE, John	Hanover	1763		401
COCKE, William	Hanover	1763		251
COKE, Saml.	James City	1768		
COKE, Samuel	James City	1768	2	
COLE, Matt.	James City	1768	2	235
COLE, Matt.	James City	1769	2	235
COLE, Thos.	James City	1768		300
COLE, William	James City	1768	2	210
COLE, William	James City	1769	2	210
COLEMAN, Benja., see Allen, Elizabeth				
COLEMAN, David, see Staples, Saml.				
COLEMAN, Johanna (mother of Ths.)	Gloucester	1770		200
Chgd. to Thomas Coleman's Est.				
COLEMAN, John	Buckingham	1774	1	
COLEMAN, John Estate	Buckingham	1774	3	
Coleman, Littleberry				
COLEMAN, Joseph	Gloucester	1770	1	

Name	County	Year	Tithables	Acres
COLEMAN, Joseph	Gloucester	1771	1	
COLEMAN, Littleberry, see Coleman, John Estate				
COLEMAN, Saml.	Buckingham	1773	3	
COLEMAN, Saml.	Buckingham	1774	2	
COLEMAN, Thos.	Hanover	1770	1	
St. Martin's Parish				
COLEMAN, Thomas, Captn.	Gloucester	1770		
COLEMAN, Thomas Est., see Coleman, Johanna				
COLEMAN, Thos. (Estate)	Gloucester	1770		566
son of Johanna - 200 Acres his mother's dower				
COLEMAN, Wm.	Gloucester	1770		
COLEMAN, Wm.	Gloucester	1771		
COLES, William	Hanover	1763		532
COLLAWN, John Senr.	Gloucester	1770	3	
COLLAWN, John Junr.	Gloucester	1770	3	
COLLAWN, John Junr.	Gloucester	1771	2	
COLLEY, Charles	Gloucester	1770		
COLLEY, William	Hanover	1763		150
COLLIAR, William	James City	1768		
COLSON, Charles - (of Luttrell)	Stafford	1768		80
from Fauquier Rental				
COLSON, Charles - (of Luttrell)	Stafford	1773		80
from Fauquier Rental				
COMBS, John	Stafford	1768		1180
COMBS, John	Stafford	1773		1330
"284 Acres sold to Wm. Hughs"				
COMPANY, ACCOKICK	Stafford	1773		2796
CONNELLY, Thos.	Gloucester	1770		
CONNELLY, Thos.	Gloucester	1771		
CONNER, Nicholas	Buckingham	1774	1	
COOK, ___ see Jewell, (Thomas)				
COOK, Elisabeth	Stafford	1768		2324
COOK, Ignatious (Kingston Parish)	Gloucester	1774	1	
COOK, Ignatious (Kingston Parish)	Gloucester	1775	1	
COOKE, Benjamin	Hanover	1763		200
COOKE, Francis Whiting	Gloucester	1770	5	
COOKE, Francis Whiting	Gloucester	1771	6	
COOKE, George	Hanover	1763		200
COOKE, Giles	Gloucester	1770	10	466½
COOKE, Giles	Gloucester	1771	11	466½
COOKE, John	Gloucester	1770	24	800
mentions his son John				
COOKE, John	Gloucester	1771	25	800
COOKE, Jno. (younger)*	Gloucester			
COOKE, John Junr.	Gloucester	1770	28	1800
(Brother of Mordecai; p. 21 says Rev. Jno. Cooke Junr.)				
COOKE, John Junr.	Gloucester	1771	27	1800
COOKE, Mordecai	Gloucester	1770	10	200
COOKE, Mordecai	Gloucester	1771	11	200
COOKE, Mordecai Junr.*	Gloucester	1770	69	
(Brother of John)				
COOKE, Mordecai Junr.	Gloucester	1771	62	
COOKE, William	Gloucester	1770	1	
COOPER, Abraham	Gloucester	1770		
COOPER, Jacob	Gloucester	1770		
COOPER, Jacob	Gloucester	1771		
COOPER, Jacob, see Bolling, Robert Jr. Col.				
COOPER, John	James City	1768	11	800
COOPER, John	James City	1769	13	800
COOPER, John	Gloucester	1770	1	

Name	County	Year	Tithables	Acres
COOPER, John	Gloucester	1771	1	
CORBIN, Francis	Stafford	1773		400
"lives in Culpeper"				
CORKER, Johanna	Gloucester	1770	4	
CORKER, Johanna	Gloucester	1771	5	
CORNWELL, Richard	Buckingham	1773	1	
CORNWELL, Richard	Buckingham	1774	1	
COROLES, William Esta.	James City	1768	4	
COSBIE, David	Hanover	1763		518
COSBIE, James	Hanover	1763	(1754)	150
COSBIE, John	Hanover	1763		718
COSBIE, John Jun.	Hanover	1763	(1757)	100
COSBY, James	James City	1769	4	
COSBEY, Overton*	Gloucester	1770		
COSBY, William (insolvent)	James City	1768	3	
COSTON, John	Hanover	1763		170
COTTEREL, Charles	Buckingham	1773	1	
COTTREL, Benjamin	Buckingham	1773	8	
Cottrel, Jacob				
COTTRELL, Benja.	Buckingham	1774	7	
Saunderson, Jno.				
COUCH, James	Buckingham	1773	1	
COUCH, James	Buckingham	1774	2	
COUCH, John	Buckingham	1773	5	
COUPLAND, Henry, see Cobbs, Thomas				
COUSINS, John, see Gibson, John				
COWLES, Thomas	James City	1768	12	419
COWLES, Thomas	James City	1769	13	419
COWNE, William	Hanover	1763		1700
Do				40
COX, John	Buckingham	1773	10	
COX, John	Buckingham	1774	10	
COX, John	Buckingham	1773		
"To John Cox the Estate of William Moseley, decd."				
Spoldin, Thomas				
COX, John	Buckingham	1774	7	
"The Estate of Moseley, William deceased"				
Spalding, Thomas				
COX, John Hartwell	Buckingham	1774	10	
Oglesby, Shadrick				
COX, Matthew	Buckingham	1773	6	
Chitwood, John				
COX, Matthew	Buckingham	1774	6	
Chitwood, John				
CRABBINS, Charles Hinson	Gloucester	1770	1	
CRAIGHEAD, William	Hanover	1763		287
CRANSHAW, William	Hanover	1770	8	700
St. Martin's Parish				
CRAP, James	Stafford	1773		290
CRAWFORD, David	Hanover	1763	(1757)	360
CRAWFORD, Richard	Hanover	1763	(1756)	100
CRAWLEY, John	James City	1768	7	318
CRAWLEY, John	James City	1769	7	318
CRAWLEY, Nathaniel	James City	1768	7	450
CRAWLEY, Nathaniel	James City	1769	8	450
CRAWLEY, William	Hanover	1763		125
CREASEY, William	Buckingham	1773	7	
Creasey, Charles				
CREASEY, William	Buckingham	1774	8	
Creasey, Charles				

Name	County	Year	Tithables	Acres
CRENSHAW, Charles	Hanover	1763		465
CREN (CREW), David	Hanover	1763		200
CRENSHAW, David	Hanover	1763		381
CRENSHAW, James	Hanover	1763		180
Do				490
CRENSHAW, Joseph	Hanover	1763		758
CRENSHAW, Nicholas	Hanover	1763		251
CRENSHAW, Susanna	Hanover	1763		338
CRENSHAW, Thomas	Hanover	1763		471
CREW, James	Hanover	1763		100
CREW, John	Gloucester	1770	1	
CREW, John	Gloucester	1771	2	
CREWS, Gideon	Buckingham	1774	1	
CREWS, Walter	Buckingham	1773	2	
Crews, Gideon				
CREWS, Walter	Buckingham	1774	2	
Crews, James				
CREYDLE, John (insolvent)	James City	1768		
CRITTENDEN, Richard	Gloucester	1770		140
CROSBY, ____, see Wood, Nehe.				
CROSBY, Uriah	Stafford	1768		350
CROSBY, Uriel	Stafford	1773		150
CROSS, James (of Chr. Hinson)	Stafford	1768		290
CROSS, Joseph	Hanover	1763		200
CROUCH, John	Buckingham	1774	5	
CRUMPTON, William	Hanover	1763		74
CRUTCHFIELD, Ralph	Hanover	1763		265
CULLEY, Christopher	Gloucester	1774	4	
Kingston Parish				
CULLEY, Christopher (Kingston Par)	Gloucester	1775	4	
CULLEY, Robert Senr.	Gloucester	1774	13	
Kingston Parish				
CULLEY, Robert Senr.	Gloucester	1775	13	
Kingston Parish				
CUMMINGER, John	Buckingham	1773	1	
CUMMINGS, John (of Smith)	Stafford	1773		40
"Lives in Fauqr."				
CUNNINGHAM, James	Buckingham	1773	2	
Cunningham, Valentine				
CUNNINGHAM, James	Buckingham	1774	3	
Cunningham, Valentine				
CUNNINGHAM, Nathaniel	Gloucester	1770	3	
CUNNINGHAM, Nathaniel	Gloucester	1771	4	
CUNNINGHAM, Valentine, see Cunningham, James				
CUMMINS, Edward	James City	1769	1	
CURD, Joseph	Buckingham	1773	9	
Curd, Charles				
CURD, Joseph	Buckingham	1774	10	
Curd, Charles				
Bradley, John				
Clark, George				
CURD, Wm., the Estate of	Buckingham	1773	5	
Epperson, Joseph Decd.				
Epperson, George				
Bailey, Yancey				
CURD, Wm.	Buckingham	1773	6	
Word, Peter				
Ambruse, Ambrose				
CURD, William	Buckingham	1774	6	
Word, Peter				

Name	County	Year	Tithables	Acres
CURREY, William	Gloucester	1770	5	95
CURREY, William	Gloucester	1771	7	95
CURRY, William Junr.	Gloucester	1770		
CUSTIS, Daniel Parks	Hanover	1763		911
CURTIS, Augustine Kingston Parish	Gloucester	1774	8	
CURTIS, Augustine Kingston Parish	Gloucester	1775	8	
CURTIS, Christopher	Gloucester	1770	7	
CURTIS, Christopher	Gloucester	1771	7	
DABNEY, Cornelius	Hanover	1763		123
DABNEY, Cornelius Jun.	Hanover	1763		150
DABNEY, John	Hanover	1763		140
DABNEY, William	Hanover	1763		800
Do				150
DADE, Baldwin	Stafford	1768		750
DADE, Baldwin	Stafford	1773		750
DADE, Cadwalader	Stafford	1773		200
DADE, Cadwallader Est.	Stafford	1768		200
DADE, Cadwallader Junr. of Charles Massey	Stafford	1768		173
DADE, Francis	Stafford	1768		200
DADE, Francis	Stafford	1773		200
DADE, Rose of Thos. Grigsby	Stafford	1768		750
DADE, Rose	Stafford	1773		950
DADE, Townshend	Stafford	1768		300
DADE, Townshend	Stafford	1773		473
DADE, Thownsend, see Addison, John				
DADE, Townsend, see Young, William				
DALBY, Nightingale	Hanover	1763		80
DALGLEISH, John Mr.	Gloucester	1771		
DALGLEISH, Robert 1771 "carried to John Dalglish Acct."	Gloucester	1770	13	490
DALGLEISH, Alexandr. Doctr.	Gloucester	1770	2	
DALGLEISH, Alexandr. Doctr.	Gloucester	1771	4	
DAMERON, George, see Staton, John				
DAMERON, Thena	Buckingham	1773	1	
DANCE, Frances	Gloucester	1770	1	
DANCE, Frances	Gloucester	1771	1	
DANCE, William	Gloucester	1770	5	
DANCE, William	Gloucester	1771	5	
DANCEY, Benjamin	James City	1768		
DANDRIDGE, Nathaniel West	Hanover	1763		7257
DANIEL, Abraham	Buckingham	1773	7	
DANIEL, Abraham	Buckingham	1774	7	
DANIEL. Peter	Stafford	1768		1800
DANIEL, Peter	Stafford	1773		1800
DANIEL, Robert	Gloucester	1770	16	1180
DANIEL, Robert	Gloucester	1771	19	1180
DANIEL, William Pride, see Trent, Alexr. Colo.				
DARNEL, Jeremiah Margaret (sic)	Gloucester	1770		34
DARRO(A)COAT	Hanover	1763		503
DARRACOAT, Thomas	Hanover	1763		500
DAVENPORT, Catherine	James City	1768	5	
DAVENPORT, Catherine	James City	1769	5	
DAVENPORT, David	Hanover	1763		75
DAVENPORT, John	Hanover	1763		75
DAVENPORT, Joseph	Gloucester	1770	12	290

Name	County	Year	Tithables	Acres
DAVENPORT, Joseph	Gloucester	1771		595
			7 Abingdon	
			5 Petsworth	
DAVENPORT, Richard	Buckingham	1774	2	
DAVIDSON, Edward, see Hoy, Wm.				
DAVIDSON, Edward Junr.	Buckingham	1774	1	
DAVIDSON, Stephen	Buckingham	1774	1	
DAVIE, Peter	Buckingham	1774	2	
Davie, Isaac, son				
DAVIE, Peter	Buckingham	1773	3	
Davie, Peter Jr.				
Davie, Isaac				
DAVIE, Peter Junr.	Buckingham	1774	1	
DAVIES, John	James City	1768	7	295
DAVIES, John	Stafford	1773		73
DAVIS, Ann Mrs.	Buckingham	1773	2	
Davis, Thos.				
DAVIS, Ann, Mrs.	Buckingham	1774	2	
Davis, Thos.				
DAVIS, Anthony	Gloucester	1770	1	
DAVIS, Anthony	Gloucester	1771	3	
(Mother - Mary Davis)				
DAVIS, Barbee	Gloucester	1770		
DAVIS, Barbee	Gloucester	1771		
DAVIS, Benja.	Buckingham	1774	1	
DAVIS, Carter (estate)	Gloucester	1770		54
DAVIS, Champness	Buckingham	1773	1	
DAVIS, Charles	Gloucester	1770		
DAVIS, Charles	Hanover	1763		100
DAVIS, Cyrus	Hanover	1763		121
DAVIS, Edward	Hanover	1763		100
DAVIS, Edward Junr.	Gloucester	1774	3	
Kingston Parish				
DAVIS, Edward Junr.	Gloucester	1775	3	
Kingston Parish				
DAVIS, George	Hanover	1763		160
DAVIS, Henry	Hanover	1763		300
DAVIS, Henry (Tillotson Par.)	Buckingham	1773	1	
DAVIS, Henry Jun.	Hanover	1763		300
DAVIS, Humphrey	Gloucester	1774	4	
Kingston Parish				
DAVIS, Humphrey	Gloucester	1775	4	
Kingston Parish				
DAVIS, Isaac Junr.	Gloucester	1774	1	
Kingston Parish				
DAVIS, Isaac Junr.	Gloucester	1775	1	
Kingston Parish				
DAVIS, Isaac Senr.	Gloucester	1774	8	
Kingston Parish				
DAVIS, Isaac Senr.	Gloucester	1775	8	
Kingston Parish				
DAVIS, James (Kingston Parish)	Gloucester	1774	17	
DAVIS, James (Kingston Parish)	Gloucester	1775	17	
DAVIS, James (Kingston Parish)	Gloucester	1774	2	
DAVIS, James (Kingston Parish)	Gloucester	1775	2	
DAVIS, Joel	Buckingham	1774	1	
DAVIS, Joel, see Cannon, John				
DAVIS, John (son) Isaac	Gloucester	1774		
DAVIS, John (son) Isaac	Gloucester	1775		

Name	County	Year	Tithables	Acres
DAVIS, John	Stafford	1768		73
DAVIS, John	James City	1769	8	295
DAVIS, John	Hanover	1763		140
DAVIS, John	James City	1768	1	75
DAVIS, John (Kingston Parish)	Gloucester	1774	3	
DAVIS, John (Kingston Parish)	Gloucester	1775	3	
DAVIS, John Senr. Kingston Parish	Gloucester	1774	1	
DAVIS, John Senr. Kingston Parish	Gloucester	1775	1	
DAVIS, John (overseer) Pd. by Peter Whiting	Gloucester	1770		
DAVIS, John Shoemaker (sic) Kingston Parish	Gloucester	1774	3	
DAVIS, John Shoemaker (sic) Kingston Parish	Gloucester	1775	3	
DAVIS, Joseph (Kingston Parish)	Gloucester	1774	3	
DAVIS, Joseph (Kingston Parish)	Gloucester	1775	3	
DAVIS, Joseph (Kingston Parish)	Gloucester	1774	1	
DAVIS, Joseph (Kingston Parish)	Gloucester	1775	1	
DAVIS, Mary	Gloucester	1770	3(Ware)	120
DAVIS, Mary	Gloucester	1771		120
DAVIS, Mathew	Buckingham	1773	1	
DAVIS, Matthew	Hanover	1763		100
DAVIS, Peter	Hanover	1763		113
DAVIS, Richard	Gloucester	1770	1	
DAVIS, Richard	Gloucester	1771	1	
DAVIS, Richd. Petsworth Parish	Gloucester	1770	6	124
DAVIS, Richd. Petsworth Parish	Gloucester	1771	6	124
DAVIS, Richard St. Martin's Parish	Hanover	1770	1	47½
DAVIS, Samuel	Gloucester	1770	1	
DAVIS, Stephen	Hanover	1763		200
Do				260
DAVIS, Thos., see Davis, Ann Mrs.				
DAVIS, Thomas (Abingdon Parish)	Gloucester	1771	1	
DAVIS, Thomas Senr. Kingston Parish	Gloucester	1774	2	
DAVIS, Thomas Senr. Kingston Parish	Gloucester	1775	2	
DAVIS, Thomas Junr. Kingston Parish	Gloucester	1774	1	
DAVIS, Thomas Junr. Kingston Parish	Gloucester	1775	1	
DAVIS, Ursula	Gloucester	1770		
DAVIS, Wm.	James City	1768		
DAVIS, William (K. William)	Hanover	1763		500
DAVIS, William, tailor	Hanover	1763		150
DAVISON, Charles	Buckingham	1773	1	
DAVISON, Edward, constable	Buckingham	1773	1	
DAVISON, Edward, "son of David Davison"	Buckingham	1773		
DAVISON, Edward, constable	Buckingham	1774	1	
DAVOCK, Charles	Hanover	1763		307
DAWS, John	James City	1768		
DAWSON, Elizabeth	James City	1768	5	
DAWSON, Elizabeth	James City	1769	6	
DAWSON, Leonard (Kingston Par.)	Gloucester	1774	1	

Name	County	Year	Tithables	Acres
DAWSON, Leonard (Kingston Par.)	Gloucester	1775	1	
DAWSON, Pricilla	James City	1768	2	
DAWSON, Priscilla	James City	1769	2	
DAWSON, Samuel	Gloucester	1770	5	198
DAWSON, Samuel	Gloucester	1771	5	198
DAY, Ambrose, see Johns, Wm. Junr.				
DAY, John	Hanover	1763		353
DAY, John	James City	1768		
DAY, John	Buckingham	1773	1	
DAY, John	Buckingham	1774	1	
DAY, Lewis	Buckingham	1773	1	
DAY, Lewis	Buckingham	1774	1	
DAY, Mary	Gloucester	1770		200
DEAN, Edeth	James City	1768		100
DEAN, Edeth	James City	1769		100
DEAN, Richd., see Watt, William				
DEAGLE, Benja.	Gloucester	1771		
DEBNAM, Charles (Kingston Parish)	Gloucester	1774	6	
DEBNAM, Charles (Kingston Parish)	Gloucester	1775	6	
DEBNAM, Thomas	Gloucester	1770	12	100
DEBNAM, Thomas	Gloucester	1771	13	100
DEBNAM, William (estate)	Gloucester	1770		47
Do				180
DEGGE, Joseph (Kingston Par.)	Gloucester	1774	12	
DEGGE, Joseph (Kingston Par.)	Gloucester	1775	12	
DEGGE, Joshua (Kingston Par.)	Gloucester	1774	1	
DEGGE, Joshua (Kingston Par.)	Gloucester	1775	1	
DEGGES, Anthony (Kingston Par.)	Gloucester	1774	3	
DEGGES, Anthony (Kingston Par.)	Gloucester	1775	3	
DEGGES, William (Kingston Par.)	Gloucester	1774	2	
DEGGES, William (Kingston Par.)	Gloucester	1775	2	
DENNIS, John	James City	1769	3	125
DENNIS, William	James City	1769	2	75
DENT, William, Exrs.	Stafford	1768		200
DENT, William	Stafford	1773		200
DENNIS, John	James City	1768	3	125
DENNIS, Matthew	James City	1768	1	75
DENNIS, William	James City	1768		
DENTON, Thomas	Hanover	1763		60
DEPRIEST, Robert	Hanover	1763		322
DEUVALL, William	Gloucester	1771	17	385
DEWS, William	Gloucester	1770	8	120
DEWS, William	Gloucester	1771	8	120
DIAL, James	Buckingham	1773	1	
DIBREL, Anthony	Buckingham	1774	7	
Dibrel, Charles				
Dibrel, John				
DIBREL, Anthony	Buckingham	1773	5	
DICKENSON, Benjamin	Hanover	1763		100
DICKENSON, Griffeth	Hanover	1763		150
DICKENSON, William	Hanover	1763		315
DICKENSON, William Jun.	Hanover	1763		150
DICKISON, Griffith (St.Martin's)	Hanover	1770	4	
DICKISON, Nathl. (St. Martin's)	Hanover	1770	4	217
DICKISON, Robert (St. Martin's)	Hanover	1770	4	
DIGGS, Dudley	James City	1768	5	660
DIGGS, Dudley	James City	1769	4	660
DIGGS, William (insolvent)	James City	1768		
DIGGS, Wm.	James City	1768		
DILLARD, John	Gloucester	1770	4	325

Name	County	Year	Tithables	Acres
DILLARD, John	Gloucester	1771	4	325
DISMUKES, James	Hanover	1763		200
DIXON, Haldenby	James City	1768	5	
DIXON, Haldenby	James City	1769	7	
DIXON, James	Gloucester	1770	9	375
DIXON, James	Gloucester	1771	9	375
DIXON, John	James City	1768		
DIXON, John (Kingston Parish)	Gloucester	1774	23	
DIXON, John (Kingston Parish)	Gloucester	1775	23	
DIXON, Thomas (Kingston Parish)	Gloucester	1774	3	
DIXON, Thomas (Kingston Parish)	Gloucester	1775	3	
DIXON, Finley (Kingston Parish)	Gloucester	1774	2	
DIXON, Finley (Kingston Parish)	Gloucester	1775	2	
DIXON, William (Kingston Parish)	Gloucester	1774	1	
DIXON, William (Kingston Parish)	Gloucester	1775	1	
DOBSON, Edmund	Gloucester	1770	7	
DOBSON, Edmund	Gloucester	1771	2	
DOBSON, Edward	Gloucester	1770	4	197
DOBSON, Edward	Gloucester	1771	4	197
DOBSON, John	Gloucester	1770	1	800
DOBSON, John	Gloucester	1771	1	800
DODD, Elizabeth	James City	1768	4	
DODD, Elizabeth	James City	1769	4	
DODD, Newcomb (Kingston Parish)	Gloucester	1774	1	
DODD, Newcomb (Kingston Parish)	Gloucester	1775	1	
DONALD, James (Tillotson Parish)	Buckingham	1773	1	
DONIPHAN, Alexander, Ex.	Stafford	1768		1176
Do				100
Do				177
DONIPHAN, Alexander, Ex.	Stafford	1773		1176
Do				100
Do				177
DONIPHAN, Matt.	Stafford	1768		650
DONIPHAN, Matt.	Stafford	1773		650
DOOLING, John, see Hughs, Ralph				
DOSS, Edward	Buckingham	1773	1	
DOSS, Edward	Buckingham	1774	1	
DOSS, James	Buckingham	1773	1	
DOSS, James	Buckingham	1774	1	
DOSS, Mark	Buckingham	1773	3	
Doss, John				
DOSS, Mark	Buckingham	1774	3	
Doss, John				
DOSS, Thomas	Buckingham	1773	1	
DOSS, Thos., Junr.	Buckingham	1774	1	
DOSWELL, Thomas	Hanover	1763		816
DOUGLAS, James	James City	1769	4	
DOUGLAS, James	Buckingham	1774	3	
Cobbs, Jesse				
DOUGLAS, John	Buckingham	1774	8	
DOUGLAS, Thomas Mother mentioned	Gloucester	1770	1	
DOUGLAS, Thomas but not named	Gloucester	1771	3	
DOUGLAS, William	Gloucester	1770	1	120
DOUGLAS, William	Gloucester	1771	2	120
DOUGLASS, Cathirn	Stafford	1768		296
of John Waller by his wife				
DOUGLASS, Cathrine	Stafford	1773		296
DOUGLASS, James	Buckingham	1773	2	
Cobbs, Jesse				
DOUGLASS, John	Buckingham	1773	7	

Name	County	Year	Tithable	Acres
DREW, Dolphin Col.	Buckingham	1773	9	
Drew, Thomas Haynes				
DREW, Dolphin Col.	Buckingham	1774	9	
Drew, Thomas Haynes				
DREWCH (?), Mary	Gloucester	1771	1	
DRIVER, John	James City	1768	1	
DRIVER, John	James City	1769	2	
DRIVER, Thomas	James City	1768	2	100
DRIVER, Thomas	James City	1769	1	100
DRUMOND, Amey	James City	1768	2	
DRUMOND, Amey	James City	1769	2	
DRUMOND, John Esta.	James City	1768	7	1025
to fees from New Kent 355				
DRUMMOND, Martha	James City	1769	7	1025
DRUMOND, William	James City	1768		
DUDLEY, George Senr.	Gloucester	1774	12	
Kingston Parish				
DUDLEY, George Senr.	Gloucester	1775	12	
Kingston Parish				
DUDLEY, George A.	Gloucester	1774	6	
Kingston Parish				
DUDLEY, George A.	Gloucester	1775	6	
Kingston Parish				
DUDLEY, John	Gloucester	1770		
DUDLEY, John	Gloucester	1771	1	
DUDLEY, Judith (Kingston Parish)	Gloucester	1774	5	
DUDLEY, Judith (Kingston Parish)	Gloucester	1775	5	
DUDLEY, Thomas	Gloucester	1770	1	150
DUDLEY, Thomas	Gloucester	1771	1	150
DUDLEY, William	Gloucester	1771	1	
DUDLEY, Williams	James City	1768	5	110
DOUGLAS, Eleanor (son Thomas)	Gloucester	1770	1	
DUGLESS, John	Gloucester	1770		
DUIGUID, Ann	Buckingham	1773	5	
Tucker, Thos.				
DUIGUID, Ann	Buckingham	1774	4	
Tucker, Thos.				
DUIGUID, Wm.	Buckingham	1773	4	
DUIGUID, Wm.	Buckingham	1774	5	
DUKE, Cleavears (St. Martin's)	Hanover	1770	40	2417
DUKE, Clivers	Hanover	1763		455
DUKE, James	Hanover	1763		415
DUKE, John	Hanover	1763		384
Do				178
DUKE, Thomas	Hanover	1763		126
DUMAS, Jeremiah	Hanover	1763		671
DUNBARR, Garven "the land your	Gloucester	1770	1	100
DUNBARR, Garven brothers"	Gloucester	1771	1	100
DUNBARR, Gowing (Kingston Par.)	Gloucester	1774	2	
DUNBARR, Gowing (Kingston Par.)	Gloucester	1775	2	
DUNCASTLE, Thomas	James City	1768	4	475
DUNCASTLE, Thomas	James City	1769	8	475
DUNCOMB, Benja. Exrs.	Stafford	1768		100
DUNHAM, James, see Saunders, Robert				
DUNKIN, James, see Dunkin, John				
DUNKIN, John	Gloucester	1770		
DUNKIN, John	Buckingham	1774	2	
Dunkin, James				
DUNLOP, Ephraim	Gloucester	1770	1	
DUNLOP, Ephraim	Gloucester	1771		

Name	County	Year	Tithables	Acres
DURFEY, Samuel	James City	1768	4	201
DURFEY, Samuel	James City	1769	3	201
DURHAM, Abraham	Hanover	1763		50
DURHAM, John	Buckingham	1773	1	
DURHAM, William	Buckingham	1773	1	
DURHAM, William	Buckingham	1774	1	
DURRAM, James, see Salley, Jacob				
DUTTON, James	Gloucester	1770		
DUVALL, William	Gloucester	1770	3	385
DYER, Sarah	James City	1768	2	
EADINS, James, see Patteson, David				
EANOS, Mary	Gloucester	1770		
EARNEST, George	James City	1769	1	
EARNEST, George	Hanover	1763		314
EASLEY, William	Buckingham	1773	2	
EASLEY, William	Buckingham	1774	5	
EASLEY, Wm.	Buckingham	1774	5	
EAST, Ezekiel	Buckingham	1774	1	
EASTER, Anne	James City	1768	3	550
EASTER, Anne	James City	1769	3	550
EDDENS, Dawson (Kingston Parish)	Gloucester	1774	3	
EDDENS, Dawson (Kingston Parish)	Gloucester	1775	3	
EDDENS, John (Kingston Parish)	Gloucester	1774	8	
EDDENS, John (Kingston Parish)	Gloucester	1775	8	
EDDENS, Samuel (Kingston Parish)	Gloucester	1774	3	
EDDENS, Samuel (Kingston Parish)	Gloucester	1775	3	
EDENS, Alexr., see Blakey, Thomas				
EDENS, James	Buckingham	1773	1	
EDINS, John	Buckingham	1773		
EDLOE, John, Esta.	James City	1768	8	646
EDWARDS, Andrew	Stafford	1768		600
EDWARDS, Andrew	Stafford	1773		600
EDWARDS, Haden	Stafford	1773		468
EDWARDS, Jesse, see Cary, Archibald Col.				
EDWARDS, John	Stafford	1773		40
EGGLESTON, Elizabeth	James City	1768	15	450
EGGLESTON, Elizabeth	James City	1769	15	450
EGGLESTON, Joseph	James City	1768	8	150
EGGLESTON, Joseph	James City	1769	9	150
EGGLESTON, William	James City	1768		
EGLESTON, Edmund	Hanover	1763		300
EGMON, Lawrance	James City	1768		
EGMON, Lawrance	James City	1769		
EIK, Lucy	Hanover	1763		62
EIK, Timothy	Hanover	1763	(1762)	125
ELDRIDGE, Rolfe Miller, David	Buckingham	1773	2	

ELDRIDGE, Rolfe
    Miller, David
    Evans, Joseph
	Buckingham	1774	4	

ELIOT, Robert	Hanover	1763		200
ELIOT, Robert Jun.	Hanover	1763		200
ELIOT, Thomas	Hanover	1763	(1762)	160
ELLETT, Zachariah, constable	Buckingham	1773		
ELLETT, Zachariah, constable	Buckingham	1774		
ELLIOTT, John Senr. Kingston Parish	Gloucester	1774	16	
ELLIOTT, John Senr.	Gloucester	1775	16	

Name	County	Year	Tithables	Acres
Kingston Parish				
ELLIOT, William	James City	1768		
ELLIOT, William	James City	1769	2	
ELLIOTT, William	Gloucester	1774	4	
Kingston Parish				
ELLIOTT, William	Gloucester	1775	4	
Kingston Parish				
ELLIS, Susanna	Hanover	1763		592
ELLSOME, Thomas	Buckingham	1774	1	
ELMORE, Peter	Hanover	1763		100
ELMORE, William	Hanover	1763		106
ELSDON, Thomas	James City	1768	8	685
ELSOM, Thomas, see Nowlin, James				
ENGLAND, Edward	Hanover	1763		252
ENOS, Lewis	Gloucester	1770	1	
ENOS, Lewis	Gloucester	1771	1	
EPPERSON, Francis	Buckingham	1774	1	
EPPERSON, George, see Curd, Wm. Estate of				
EPPERSON, George, see Curd, Wm. Est. of Joseph Epperson dec'd				
EPPERSON, Joseph, dec'd, see Curd, William Estate of				
EPPERSON, Littleberry	Buckingham	1773	3	
Woodward, Jeremiah				
EPPERSON, Littleberry	Buckingham	1774	3	
Woodward, Jeremiah				
EPPERSON, Paul	Hanover	1763		108
ESTHER, Richard	Gloucester	1770		
ESTHER, William	Gloucester	1770	2	35
ESTHER, William	Gloucester	1771	2	35
ETHERAGE, William	James City	1769	1	
ETHERINGTON, Daniel (of Pratt)	Stafford	1773		100
ETHRINGTON, William	Stafford	1768		749
ETHRINGTON, William	Stafford	1773		749
EUSTACE, Isaac	Stafford	1768		600
EUSTACE, Isaac	Stafford	1773		850
EVANS, Elizabeth (Kingston Parish)	Gloucester	1774		
EVANS, Elizabeth (Kingston Parish)	Gloucester	1775		
EVANS, Joseph, see Eldridge, Rolfe				
EVANS, Joseph, see Mosley, Francis				
EVANS, Lewis (Kingston Parish)	Gloucester	1774	1	
EVANS, Lewis (Kingston Parish)	Gloucester	1775	1	
EVANS, Robert	Buckingham	1773	1	
EVANS, Robert	Buckingham	1774	1	
EVANS, William	Gloucester	1774	1	
Kingston Parish				
EVANS, William	Gloucester	1775	1	
Kingston Parish				
EVERARD, Thomas	James City	1768	9	600
EVERARD, Thomas	James City	1769	8	
EVINS, Thomas	Buckingham	1773	1	
EVITT, Nehamiah	Buckingham	1773	1	
EVITT, Thomas	Buckingham	1773	1	
FALWELL, Henry, see Moss, Thomas				
FALWELL, Wm.	Buckingham	1774	2	
Falwell, James				
FANNING, Harry, see Ridgeway, Phebey				
FANTLEROY, William	Hanover	1763		3433
FARDING, Mary	James City	1769	1	50
FARDING, William	James City	1769	3	

Name	County	Year	Tithables	Acres
FARGUSON, Edward	Buckingham	1773	1	
FARGUSON, Joel	Buckingham	1773	1	
FARGUSON, John	Buckingham	1773	1	
FARGUSON, John	Buckingham	1774	2	
FARGUSON, Moses	Buckingham	1773	1	
FARGUSON, Wm.	Buckingham	1773	1	
FARMER, William	Hanover	1763		300
FARTHING, Mary	James City	1768	1	50
FARTHING, William	James City	1768	3	
FARTHING, Wm. (insolvent)	James City	1768	1	
FARY, George	Gloucester	1770		50
FARY, Robert	Gloucester	1770		50
FEAR, Hamner	James City	1768	3	90
FEAR, Hamner	James City	1769	3	90
FEAR, William (insolvent)	James City	1768	1	
FEARN, John	Buckingham	1773	8	
FEARN, John	Buckingham	1774	7	
FEARN, Thomas Furlong, John	Buckingham	1773	4	
FEARN, Thomas Furlong, John	Buckingham	1774	5	
FENTON, Robert	Hanover	1763		100
FERGUSON, Edward	Buckingham	1774	1	
FERGUSON, Joel	Buckingham	1771	1	
FERGUSON, John	Buckingham	1774	1	
FERGUSON, Moses	Buckingham	1774	1	
FERGUSON, Wm.	Buckingham	1774	1	
FIELD, John (St. Martin's)	Hanover	1770	4	120
FIELDS, (Joh)n (Mulatto)	Buckingham	1774	1	
FIELDE, Thomas (Kingston Parish)	Gloucester	1774	11	
FIELDE, Thomas (Kingston Parish)	Gloucester	1775	11	
FIGG, James	Gloucester	1771	1	
FIGG, John Junr.	Gloucester	1770	1	
FIGG, John Senr. (Ware)	Gloucester	1770	5	273
FIGG, John Senr. (Ware)	Gloucester	1771	5	273
FIGG, Matthew	Gloucester	1770	2	
FIGG, Matthew	Gloucester	1771	3	
FIGG, Matthew Junr.	Gloucester	1770	1	
FIGG, Matthew Junr.	Gloucester	1771	1	
FIGG, William	Gloucester	1771	1	
FINCH, Ralph	Hanover	1763	(1755)	290
FINNEY, William	Gloucester	1770	4	
FINNEY, William	Gloucester	1771	7	
FISHER, David	James City	1768	3	75
FISHER, David	James City	1769	4	75
FISHER, Thomas	James City	1768	1	
FISHER, Thomas	James City	1769	2	
FISHER, William	James City	1768	2	50
FISHER, William	James City	1769	2	50
FITCHAWALD, John, see Webb, Theodorick				
FITCHETT, Daniel (Kingston Par.)	Gloucester	1774	6	
FITCHETT, Daniel (Kingston Par.)	Gloucester	1775	6	
FITCHET, Thomas (Kingston Par.)	Gloucester	1774	1	
FITCHET, Thomas (Kingston Parish)	Gloucester	1775	1	
FITZHUGH, ____, see Hansbrough, Peter				
FITZHUGH, Henry Col.	Stafford	1768		4041
Do				10067
Do		of Churchill--		2370
FITZHUGH, Henry Col.	Stafford	1773		16678
FITZHUGH, Henry Jr.	Stafford	1773		533

Name	County	Year	Tith-ables	Acres
FITZHUGH, John	James City	1768	3	100
FITZHUGH, John	Stafford	1768		1250
FITZHUGH, John	Stafford	1773		1261
FITZHUGH, Martha	James City	1769	3	100
FITZHUGH, Thomas	James City	1768	2	
FITZHUGH, Thomas, Exrs.	Stafford	1768		600
FITZHUGH, Thomas, Exrs.	Stafford	1773		600
FITZHUGH, William, Esqr.	Stafford	1768		23975
FITZHUGH, William, Esqr.	Stafford	1773		23975
FITZHUGH, William (Maryland)	Stafford	1768		5575
(2035 Acres in P. William)				
FITZHUGH, William Sr., Esq.	Stafford	1768		3300
FITZHUGH, William Senr.	Stafford	1773		3035
(708 Acres sold to John Stuart)				
FLECHER, Ann (Kingston Parish)	Gloucester	1774		
FLECHER, Ann (Kingston Parish)	Gloucester	1775		
FLEMING, Charles	Gloucester	1770		
FLEMING, John	Gloucester	1770		
FLEMING, John	Gloucester	1771		
FLEMING, Thomas	Gloucester	1771	1	
FLEMMING, William	Gloucester	1770	5	350
FLEMMING, William	Gloucester	1771		269
FLETCHER, Benja.	Gloucester	1770	1	
FLETCHER, Benja.	Gloucester	1771		
FLETCHER, Charles	Gloucester	1770		
FLETCHER, Henry	Gloucester	1770	1	
FLETCHER, Nathaniel	Gloucester	1770	4	228
FLETCHER, Nathani	Gloucester	1771	4	228
FLETCHER, Sarah	Stafford	1768		90
FLETCHER, Sarah	Stafford	1773		90
FLIPING, Humphrey Kingston Parish	Gloucester	1774	1	
FLIPING, Humphrey Kingston Parish	Gloucester	1775	1	
FLIPPIN, John (Kingston Parish)	Gloucester	1774	3	
FLIPPIN, John (Kingston Parish)	Gloucester	1775	3	
FLIPPIN, Thomas (Kingston Parish)	Gloucester	1774	10	
FLIPPIN, Thomas (Kingston Parish)	Gloucester	1775	10	
FLOOD, Henry, see Ayres, Samuel				
FLOOD, John	Buckingham	1774	1	
FLOOD, William	James City	1768		
FLUD, John	Buckingham	1773	1	
FLOWERS, Andrew (Tillotson Parish)	Buckingham	1773	1	
FLOWERS, Andw.	Buckingham	1774	1	
FLOWERS, Ralph (Tillotson Parish)	Buckingham	1773	1	
FLOWERS, Ralph	Buckingham	1774	2	
FOARD, Richd.	Buckingham	1774	1	
FOLKS, Gabriel	Hanover	1763		375
FOOTE, Richard	Stafford	1768		400
FOOTE, Richard	Stafford	1773		400
Now the Revd. Will. Stuart's				
FORD, Boaz	Buckingham	1773	1	
FORD, Boaz	Buckingham	1774	1	
FORD, Eliza, see Ford, John				
FORD, James (Levy Free)	Buckingham	1773	1	
FORD, James	Buckingham	1774	1	
FORD, James, Junr.	Buckingham	1773	1	
FORD, James, Junr.	Buckingham	1774	1	
FORD, John and Eliza	Hanover	1763		150
Do				125

Name	County	Year	Tithables	Acres
FORD, William	Hanover	1763		150
FORDE, Richard	Buckingham	1773	1	
FORREST, Abraham Junr. Kingston Parish	Gloucester	1774	1	
FORREST, Abraham Junr. Kingston Parish	Gloucester	1775	1	
FORREST, George (Kingston Parish)	Gloucester	1774	1	
FORREST, George (Kingston Parish)	Gloucester	1775	1	
FORREST, George Junr. Kingston Parish	Gloucester	1774	1	
FORREST, George Junr. Kingston Parish	Gloucester	1775	1	
FORREST, George Senr. Kingston Parish	Gloucester	1774	3	
FORREST, George Senr. Kingston Parish	Gloucester	1775	3	
FORREST, Henry (Kingston Parish)	Gloucester	1774	4	
FORREST, Henry (Kingston Parish)	Gloucester	1775	4	
FORREST, John Junr. Kingston Parish	Gloucester	1774	1	
FORREST, John Junr. Kingston Parish	Gloucester	1775	1	
FORREST, John Senr. Kingston Parish	Gloucester	1774	3	
FORREST, John Senr. Kingston Parish	Gloucester	1775	3	
FORREST, Philip (Kingston Parish)	Gloucester	1774	1	
FORREST, Philip (Kingston Parish)	Gloucester	1775	1	
FORSIE, John	Hanover	1763	(1759)	150
FOSTER, Franics (Kingston Parish)	Gloucester	1774	1	
FOSTER, Francis (Kingston Parish)	Gloucester	1775	1	
FOSTER, Isaac (Kingston Parish)	Gloucester	1774	3	
FOSTER, Isaac (Kingston Parish)	Gloucester	1775	3	
FOSTER, Jassey (Kingston Par.)	Gloucester	1774	1	
FOSTER, Jassey (Kingston Par.)	Gloucester	1775	1	
FOSTER, Joel (Kingston Par.)	Gloucester	1774	5	
FOSTER, Joel (Kingston Par.)	Gloucester	1775	5	
FOSTER, John	Gloucester	1770	6	
FOSTER, John	Gloucester	1771	6	
FOSTER, John (Kingston Par.)	Gloucester	1774	1	
FOSTER, John (Kingston Par.)	Gloucester	1775	1	
FOSTER, John Junr. Kingston Parish	Gloucester	1774	6	
FOSTER, John Junr. Kingston Parish	Gloucester	1775	6	
FOSTER, John Senr. Kingston Parish	Gloucester	1774	6	
FOSTER, John Senr. Kingston Parish	Gloucester	1775	6	
FOSTER, Joshua (Kingston Par.)	Gloucester	1774	5	
FOSTER, Joshua (Kingston Par.)	Gloucester	1775	5	
FOSTER, Josiah (Kingston Par.)	Gloucester	1774	5	
FOSTER, Josiah (Kingston Par.)	Gloucester	1775	5	
FOSTER, Mary	Gloucester	1770	11	600
FOSTER, Mary	Gloucester	1771	11	600
FOSTER, Mary	Gloucester	1770	5	30
FOSTER, Mary	Gloucester	1771	5	30
FOSTER, Richard	Hanover	1763		140
FOSTER, Robert (Kingston Par.)	Gloucester	1774	7	
FOSTER, Robert (Kingston Par.)	Gloucester	1775	7	

Name	County	Year	Tithables	Acres
FOSTER, Robert (Kingston Par.)	Gloucester	1774	1	
FOSTER, Robert (Kingston Par.)	Gloucester	1775	1	
FOSTER, Thomas	Gloucester	1770	6	
FOSTER, Thomas	Gloucester	1771	7	
FOSTER, William (Kingston Par.)	Gloucester	1774	1	
FOSTER, William (Kingston Par.)	Gloucester	1775	1	
FOULKS, Keen	James City	1769		
FOUNTAIN, Peter	Hanover	1763		775
FOUSHEE, Francis	Stafford	1773		228
FOWKE, Chandler	Stafford	1768		500
FOWKE, Chandler	Stafford	1773		500
FOWKE, Gerrard	Stafford	1768		1134
FOWKE, Gerrard, Exrs.	Stafford	1773		834
FOWKE, Gerrard, see Massey, Thomas				
FOWKE, Richard	Stafford	1768		500
FOWKE, Richard	Stafford	1773		500
FOWLEY, John	Stafford	1768		500
FOWLEY, John	Stafford	1773		500
FOX, Benjamin	James City	1768	6	110
FOX, Benjamin	James City	1769	6	110
FOX, John	Gloucester	1770	13)	3150
		1770	37)	
FOX, John	Gloucester	1771		3150
FOX, John, Senr.	Gloucester	1770		
FOX, Samuel	James City	1768		
FRANCIS, Wm.	Buckingham	1774	1	
FRANCIS, Wm., see Webb, Wm.				
FRANKLIN, Hen:, see Grisham, Lee				
FRASER, Jeremiah	Hanover	1763		300
FRAZIER, Philemon	Hanover	1763		102
FREELAND, Mace Pendleton, Ben	Buckingham	1773	5	

FREELAND, Mace
  Freland, Mace
  Pendleton, John
	Buckingham	1774	5	

FREEMAN, Charles	Gloucester	1770	1	
FREEMAN, Charles	Gloucester	1771	3	
FREEMAN, James	Gloucester	1770		
FREEMAN, Joseph	James City	1769	2	
FREEMAN, Joseph (insolvent)	James City	1768	2	
FREEMAN, Richard	Gloucester	1770	1	
FREEMAN, Thomas Junr.	Gloucester	1770		
FRELAND, Mace, see Freeland, Mace				
FRELAND, Robt. Harris, John	Buckingham	1773	4	
FRISTOE, Daniel	Stafford	1768		100
FRISTOE, Daniel	Stafford	1773		100
FRISTOE, John	Stafford	1768		100
FRISTOE, John	Stafford	1773		100
FRISTOE, Richard	Stafford	1768		174
FRISTOE, Richard	Stafford	1773		174
FRITTER, Moses of H. Horton	Stafford	1768		50
FRITTER, Moses of H. Horton	Stafford	1773		50
FUQUA, Joseph	Buckingham	1774	1	
FUQUA, Joseph, see Fuqua, Wm.				
FUQUA, William Fuqua, Wm., Jr.	Buckingham	1774	3	

FUQUA, Wm.
  Fuqua, Joseph
  Fuqua, Wm.
	Buckingham	1773	4	

Name	County	Year	Tith-ables	Acres
FURLONG, John, see Fearn, Thomas				
FURLONG, Robert, see Langhorn, Morris				
GADDES, Alexr. & C., see Brent, Robert				
GAIRDNER, John	Hanover	1763		200
GAIRDNER, William	Hanover	1763		130
GALLAHON, Terry, see Gibson, Edward				
GALLAWAY, Wm.	Buckingham	1774		
GALLE, Terry	Buckingham	1774	1	
GANNAWAY, John Jr.	Buckingham	1773	7	
Gannaway, Gregory				
GANNAWAY, John Junr.	Buckingham	1774	6	
Gannaway, Gregory				
GANNAWAY, John yr. (younger)	Buckingham	1774	4	
Woodson, John				
Morgan, Edward				
Johnson, Richd.				
GANNAWAY, John Senr.	Buckingham	1773	7	
GANNAWAY, Wm.	Buckingham	1774	3	
Bryam, Henry				
GARDINER, George	Gloucester	1770	6	160
GARDINER, George	Gloucester	1771	4	160
GARDNER, Zach.*	Gloucester	1770		
GARLAND, Edward	Hanover	1763	(1755)	900
GARLAND, John (son of Peter)	Hanover	1763	(1755)	800
GARLAND, John Park	Hanover	1763		400
GARLAND, Peter, see Garland, John				
GARLAND, Peter (of B. Neck)	Hanover	1763		100
GARLAND, Robert Estate	Gloucester	1770	9	300
(300 A. bought of Guttery)				
GARLAND, Robert Estate	Gloucester	1771	9	300
(300 A. bought of Guttery)				
GARLAND, Robert	Hanover	1770	8	998
St. Martin's Parish				
GARNETT, Edwin, see Johns, Jesse				
GARRATT, Charles, dec'd, Estate of	Buckingham	1774	5	
Pasley, Richard				
GARRATT, Stephen	Buckingham	1774	2	
Garratt, John				
GARRATT, Thomas	Buckingham	1773	1	
GARRETT, John, see Bolling, Archibald				
GARROTT, Charles	Buckingham	1773	6	
Thomson, Wm.				
GARROTT, Henry, see Cary, Archibald Col.				
GARROTT, John, see Garrott, Stephen				
GARROTT, John, see Webb, Theodrick				
GARROTT, Stephen	Buckingham	1773	3	
Garrott, John				
Rakes, Charles				
GARTHARD, John B., see Bradley, Wm.	Buckingham	1774		
GATES, Charles	Buckingham	1773	1	
GATES, Charles	Buckingham	1774	2	
Gates, Hezekiah				
GATES, Elijah, see Gates, William				
GATES, Hezekiah, see Gates, Charles				
GATES, William	Buckingham	1773	4	
Gates, Elijah				
GATES, William	Buckingham	1774	4	

Name	County	Year	Tithables	Acres
Gates, Elijah				
GAYLE, Catherene (Kingston Par.)	Gloucester	1774	3	
GAYLE, Catherene (Kingston Par.)	Gloucester	1775	3	
GAYLE, Christopher, Estate Kingston Parish	Gloucester	1774	7	
GAYLE, Christopher, Estate Kingston Parish	Gloucester	1775	7	
GAYLE, George (Kingston Parish)	Gloucester	1774	2	
GAYLE, George (Kingston Parish)	Gloucester	1775	2	
GAYLE, John (Kingston Parish)	Gloucester	1774	5	
GAYLE, John (Kingston Parish)	Gloucester	1775	5	
GAYLE, Matthew (Kingston Par.)	Gloucester	1774	2	
GAYLE, Matthew (Kingston Par.)	Gloucester	1775	2	
GAYLE, Matthias, Estate Kingston Parish	Gloucester	1774	2	
GAYLE, Matthias, Estate Kingston Parish	Gloucester	1775	2	
GAYLE, Robert (Kingston Par.)	Gloucester	1774	4	
GAYLE, Robert (Kingston Par.)	Gloucester	1775	4	
GAYLE, Sarah (Kingston Parish)	Gloucester	1774	2	
GAYLE, Sarah (Kingston Parish)	Gloucester	1775	2	
GEDDY, Anne	James City	1768	1	100
GEDDY, Anne	James City	1769	1	100
GEDDY, James	James City	1768		
GEDDY, Richard	James City	1768	5	125
GEDDY, Richard	James City	1769	5	125
GEDDY, William	James City	1768	6	326
GEDDY, William	James City	1769	5	150
GENKINS, John	Buckingham	1774	1	
GENKINS, Joseph Junr.	Buckingham	1774	1	
GENKINS, Joseph Senr.	Buckingham	1774	1	
GENTREY, Aaron	Hanover	1763		63
GENTREY, James	Hanover	1763		776
GENTREY, Joseph	Hanover	1763		70
GENTRY, George	Hanover	1763		100
GEORGE, Nichs.	Stafford	1768		227
GEORGE, Nichs.	Stafford	1773		227
GEORGE, Nichs.	Stafford	1768		200
GEORGE, Nichs.	Stafford	1773		200
GEORGE, William, see King, Elisabeth				
GERRARD, James	Hanover	1763		200
GERRARD, Wm. of Hum. Pope	Stafford	1768		200
GERRARD, William	Stafford	1773		200
GIBSON, Benjamine, see Berryman, John				
GIBSON, Edward Gallahon, Terry	Buckingham	1773	5	
GIBSON, Edward Gibson, John	Buckingham	1774	5	
GIBSON, Henry	Gloucester	1770	1	
GIBSON, John Cousins, John	Buckingham	1773	2	
GIBSON, John, see Gibson, Edward				
GIBSON, Miles	Buckingham	1774	2	
GIBSON, William	Buckingham	1773	2	
GIBSON, William	Buckingham	1774	1	
GIBSON, Wm.	Buckingham	1774	4	
GIDEON, Francis, see Murrow, Jno. Senr.				
GILBERT, Henry	Hanover	1763		882
GILCHRIST & CO.	James City	1768		
GILCHRIST, John	Hanover	1763		143

Name	County	Year	Tith-ables	Acres
GILLES, John	Hanover	1763		119
GILLEY, Francis	Buckingham	1773	5	
Gilley, Charles				
Gilley, Francis				
GILLIAM, Archr., see Patteson, Thomas				
GILLIAM, Charles	Buckingham	1774	1	
GILLIAM, John	Buckingham	1773	4	
GILLIAM, John	Buckingham	1774	5	
GILLIAM, Mary	Hanover	1763		300
GILLIAM, William	Hanover	1763		280
GILLIAM, Wm.	Buckingham	1774	3	
GILMAN, Richard	Hanover	1763		100
GILMORE, George	James City	1768	3	
GILMORE, George	James City	1769	5	
GIST, Samuel	Hanover	1763		2400
Do		1762		560

  "Purchased of Mills   1710
      Do   of Chiles   50
      Do   of Jones   200
                         1960 Acres
  Wife's dower int. 320-1/3
  This dower went away at 400
  my wife's death   2400"

Name	County	Year	Tith-ables	Acres
GLASCOCK, Abraham	Gloucester	1774	1	
Kingston Parish				
GLASCOCK, Abraham (Kingston Par.)	Gloucester	1775	1	
GLASCOCK, Isaac (Kingston Par.)	Gloucester	1774		
GLASCOCK, Isaac (Kingston Par.)	Gloucester	1775	1	
GLASS, David	Hanover	1763	(1759)	200
GLASS, Mary	Gloucester	1770		
GLASS, Richard	Hanover	1763	(1761)	172
GLASS, Thomas's orphans	Hanover	1763		200
GLEE (sic) LAND	Stafford	1773		664
GLEEB (sic) for the poor	Stafford	1773		100
GLEN, James	Hanover	1763		300
GLEN, John	Hanover	1763		385
GLEN, John Jun.	Hanover	1763	(1759)	100
GLEN, Josias	Hanover	1763	(1759)	125
GLEN, Lucy	Hanover	1763	(1759)	33
GLEN, Matthew	Hanover	1763		100
GLOVER, Anthy, see Glover, Samuel				
GLOCER, Edmond, see Glover, Robert				
GLOVER, Edmond	Buckingham	1774	2	
GLOVER, John	Buckingham	1773	8	
Glover, John Jr.				
GLOVER, John	Buckingham	1774	9	
Glover, John Jr.				
GLOVER, John Jr.	Buckingham	1773	3	
Harris, James				
GLOVER, John Jr.	Buckingham	1774	3	
GLOVER, Joseph	Buckingham	1773	1	
GLOVER, Robert	Buckingham	1773	10	
Glover, Edmond				
GLOVER, Robt.	Buckingham	1774	10	
GLOVER, Saml., see Goff, William				
GLOVER, Samuel	Buckingham	1773	12	
Griffin, Zachariah				
Glover, Anthy.				
GLOVER, Samuel	Buckingham	1774	12	
GLOVER, Samuel, Jur.	Buckingham	1774	1	

Name	County	Year	Tithables	Acres
GODFREE, John	Buckingham	1774	1	
GODSAY, Augustine, see Godsay, Thomas				
GODSAY, Henry, see Moseley, John				
GODSEY, Austin, see Godsey, Thomas				
GODSEY, Thomas	Buckingham	1773	2	
Godsey, Austin				
GODSAY, Thomas	Buckingham	1773	2	
Godsay, Augustine				
GODSAY, Thomas	Buckingham	1774	2	
Godsay, Augustine				
GODWIN, Elizabeth	Hanover	1763		350
GODWIN, James	Hanover	1763		749
GODWIN, John	Hanover	1763		260
Do				215
GODWIN, Thomas	Hanover	1763		200
GOING, James	Gloucester	1770		
GOING, James	Gloucester	1771		
GOING, Philip	Hanover	1763		220
GOINGS, Moses, see Cloar, John				
GOOCH, John	Hanover	1763		97
GOOCH, William Esqr.	Hanover	1763		465
GOOD, William	James City	1768	2	50
GOOD, William	James City	1769	2	50
GOODALL, Charles	Hanover	1763		677
GOODALL, Charles	James City	1768	4	250
GOODALL, Charles	James City	1769	5	250
GOODALL, John	James City	1768	2	49
GOODALL, John	James City	1769	2	49
GOODALL, John	James City	1768		
GOODALL, John	James City	1769	1	50
GOODALL, William	James City	1768	1	50
GOODALL, William	James City	1769	2	50
GOODMAN, Benjamin	Hanover	1763		50
GOODMAN, Joseph	Hanover	1763		200
GOODMAN, Robert	Hanover	1763		170
GOODMAN, Samuel	Hanover	1763		925
GOODWIN, Ann	James City	1768	1	214
GOODWIN, Robert	James City	1768	3	
GOODWIN, Robert	James City	1769	2	214
GOTT, William	Buckingham	1773	2	
Glover, Saml.				
GOOLDSBY, Charles, see Cannon, John				
GOOLSBY, Daniel, see Jordon, Samuel				
GORDON, Motley (mulatto)	Buckingham	1774	1	
GORDON, Northly	Buckingham	1773	1	
GOSLING, John	Hanover	1763		40
GOSS, Benjamin	Buckingham	1773	1	
GOSS, James	Buckingham	1773	6	
Railey, Shelton				
GOSS, James	Buckingham	1774	6	
Railey, Shelton				
GOTHARD, John, see Whitney, Jeremiah				
GOUGH, Thomas	Stafford	1768		200
GOUCH, Thomas	Stafford	1773		200
GOWING, Wm., see Williams, Robt.				
GRADY, William	Stafford	1768		100
GRADY, William	Stafford	1773		100
GRAINGER, Catherine	James City	1768	1	
"moved out of the county"				
GRANT, Alexander	Hanover	1763		140

Name	County	Year	Tithables	Acres
GRANT, Andrew of Scott	Stafford	1773		220
GRANT, Thomas	Hanover	1763		800
GRANTLAND, James	Hanover	1763	(1759)	100
GRAVES, John	Gloucester	1770	1	
GRAVES, Joseph (St. Martin's Par.)	Hanover	1770	2	93
GRAVES, Mary	Hanover	1763	(1761)	200
GRAVES, Richard (insolvent)	James City	1768		
GRAVES, Thomas Junr.	Gloucester	1770	1	
GRAVES, Thomas Senr.	Gloucester	1770	5	50
GRAVES, Thomas Senr.	Gloucester	1771	5	50
GRAVES, William	Hanover	1763		200
GRAVES, William	Gloucester	1770	1	
GRAVES, William	Gloucester	1771	1	
GRAY, George Exrs.	Stafford	1768		415
150 Acres of Anthony Kitchin				
GRAY, George Exrs.	Stafford	1773		700
GRAY, John	Hanover	1763		206
GREEN, Caleb	Stafford	1768		200
GREEN, Caleb	Stafford	1773		200
GREEN, Elizabeth (Kingston Par.)	Gloucester	1774		
GREEN, Elizabeth (Kingston Par.)	Gloucester	1775		
GREEN, Filmer	James City	1768	14	280
GREEN, Filmer	James City	1769	13	280
"to Quit 100 acres for son Walker"				
GREEN, George, (Ex. of Geo. A. Dudley)	Gloucester	1770	14	500
GREEN, George, (Ex. of Geo. A. Dudley)	Gloucester	1771	14	500
GREEN, George, see Green, William				
GREEN, James (Kingston Parish)	Gloucester	1774	1	
GREEN, James (Kingston Parish)	Gloucester	1775	1	
GREEN, John (Kingston Parish)	Gloucester	1774	2	
GREEN, John (Kingston Parish)	Gloucester	1775	2	
GREEN, John Junr. (Kingston Par.)	Gloucester	1774	1	
GREEN, John, Junr.	Gloucester	1775	1	
Kingston Parish				
GREEN, Joseph, see Stephens, John				
GREEN, Richard (Kingston Par.)	Gloucester	1774	3	
GREEN, Richard (Kingston Par.)	Gloucester	1775	3	
GREEN, Thomas	Hanover	1763		297
GREEN, Simon (Kingston Parish)	Gloucester	1774	1	
GREEN, Simon (Kingston Parish)	Gloucester	1775	1	
GREEN, William*	Gloucester	1770		
Brother of G(eorge)				
GREEN, William (Kingston Parish)	Gloucester	1774	1	
GREEN, William (Kingston Parish)	Gloucester	1775	1	
GREENHOW, John	James City	1768	4	96
GREENHOW, John	James City	1769	6	96
GREENLEES, William	Stafford	1768		400
GREENLEES & ORR	Stafford	1773		400
GREGORY, Peter	Hanover	1763		71
GREGORY, Richard	Gloucester	1771	16	326
Iverson, Gregory Estate				
GREGORY, Richard	Gloucester	1770	14	1398
Exrs. James Morris, of 326 Acres of Gregory Iverson's Est.				
GREGORY, Richard	Gloucester	1771		1398
Exrs. James Morris, of 326 Acres of Gregory Iverson's Est.				
GREGORY, William	Buckingham	1773	6	
Gregory, Thomas				
GREGORY, Wm.	Buckingham	1774	6	

Name	County	Year	Tithables	Acres
Gregory, Thomas				
GRIFFIN, Edward	Gloucester	1770	1	
GRIFFIN, Henry	Gloucester	1770		
GRIFFIN, Henry	Gloucester	1771		
GRIFFIN, Thomas	Gloucester	1770		
GRIFFIN, Zachariah, see Glover, Samuel				
GRIGG, John	Stafford	1768		520
GRIGG, John	Stafford	1773		432
"Sold to Wishart's Exrs."				
GRIGSBY, ____, see Marques, Jno.				
GRIGSBY, John, see Raley, William				
GRIGSBY, Rueben	Stafford	1768		90
GRIGSBY, Thos., see Dade, Rose				
GRIGSBY, William	Stafford	1768		300
GRIGSBY, William, Exrs.	Stafford	1773		300
GRIGSBY, William, see Raley, William				
GRIMES, John (returned insolvent)	James City	1768	2	
GRIMES, William	Hanover	1763		500
GRISHAM, Lee	Buckingham	1774	2	
Franklin, Hen:				
GRISSETT, Francis	Gloucester	1770	1	
GRISSETT, Francis	Gloucester	1771	2	
GRISSETT, James	Gloucester	1770	3	75
GRISSETT, James	Gloucester	1771	3	75
GRISSETT, John	Gloucester	1770	2	85
GRISSETT, John	Gloucester	1771	3	85
GRUBBS, John	Hanover	1763		500
GRUBBS, Thomas	Hanover	1763		230
GRUMBLY, Francis	Gloucester	1770	2	
GRUMBLY, Francis	Gloucester	1771	2	
GRUMBLY, Swan	Gloucester	1770	1	
GRUMBLY, Swan	Gloucester	1771	1	
GRYMES, Mary	James City	1768	14	
GRYMES, Phill (Estate)	Gloucester	1770	25	1620
GRYMES, Phill (Estate)	Gloucester	1771	27	1620
GUANAWAY, John Senr.	Buckingham	1774	7	
GUERRANT, Peter	Buckingham	1773	3	
GUERRANT, Peter	Buckingham	1774	4	
Guerrant, Jno.				
GUILLERY, Francis	Buckingham	1774	5	
Guillery, Charles				
Guillery, Francis				
GUTTERY, see Garland, Robert Estate				
GUTTERY, John	James City	1768		
GUTTERY, John	Gloucester	1770	2	27
GUTTERY, John	Gloucester	1771	3	27
GWYN, Hugh (Kingston Parish)	Gloucester	1774	15	
GWYN, Hugh (Kingston Parish)	Gloucester	1775	15	
GWYN, Humphrey (Kingston Parish)	Gloucester	1774	16	
GWYN, Humphrey (Kingston Parish)	Gloucester	1775	16	
HADEN, Anthony	Hanover	1763		200
HADIN, John's Exors.	Hanover	1763	(1755)	580
HADIN, Thomas	Hanover	1763		200
HAINCOCK, Robert	Buckingham	1773	1	
HAINES, Christopher	Hanover	1763		348
HAINES, Daniel	Gloucester	1770	1	
HAINES, David	Hanover	1763		144
HAINES, Edward (insolvent)	James City	1768	1	

Name	County	Year	Tith-ables	Acres
HAINES, George, Junr.	Gloucester	1770	1	
HAINES, George, Junr.	Gloucester	1771	1	
HAINES, George Junr.	Gloucester	1770	1	
HAINES, George Junr.	Gloucester	1771	1	
HAINES, John	Hanover	1763		200
HAINES, John	Gloucester	1770	4	100
HAINES, John	Gloucester	1771	2	100
HAINES, Thomas	Hanover	1763		205
HAINES, William	Hanover	1763		270
HAINES, William	Gloucester	1770		150
HAIRFIELD, Michael	James City	1768	2	50
HAIRFIELD, Michael	James City	1769	2	50
HALEY, Mary	Gloucester	1770	1	
HALEY, Mary	Gloucester	1771	1	
HALL, Beverly	Gloucester	1770	1	
HALL, Charles	Buckingham	1774	1	
HALL, Henry	Hanover	1763		130
HALL, Henry	Gloucester	1770	4	100
HALL, Henry	Gloucester	1771	3	100
HALL, James	Hanover	1763		50
HALL, John (Capt. Whiting's overseer)	Gloucester	1770		
HALL, John	Gloucester	1770	12	385
HALL, John	Gloucester	1771	13	385
HALL, John	Gloucester	1770	8	215
HALL, John	Gloucester	1771	10	215
HALL, John (Petsworth Parish)*	Gloucester	1770		
HALL, John (Petsworth Parish)*	Gloucester	1771		
HALL, John (St. Martin's Parish)	Hanover	1770	3	100
HALL, Joseph	Gloucester	1770	3	
HALL, Joseph	Gloucester	1771	3	
HALL, Lewis	Gloucester	1771		
HALL, Richard	Gloucester	1770	2	
HALL, Richard	Gloucester	1771	2	
HALL, Sarah	Gloucester	1770		60
HALL, Sarah	Gloucester	1771		60
HALL, Solomon	Gloucester	1770		150
HALL, Solomon	Gloucester	1771	1	150
HALL, Stephen	Gloucester	1771	1	
HALL, Thomas	Gloucester	1770	3	
HALL, Thomas	Gloucester	1771	5	
HALL, Thomas (Kingston Parish)	Gloucester	1774		
HALL, Thomas (Kingston Parish)	Gloucester	1775		
HALL, William	Hanover	1763	(1757)	130
HALL, William	Buckingham	1773	1	
HALL, William	Gloucester	1770	9	634
HALL, William	Gloucester	1771	10	
HALL, Wm. Jur.	Buckingham	1774	1	
HAMBLET, Archer, see Jordan, Reuben				
HAMILTON, Arthur	Gloucester	1770	1	325
HAMILTON, Arthur	Gloucester	1771		325
HAMILTON, Morris	Buckingham	1773	1	
HAMILTON, Morris	Buckingham	1774	1	
HAMILTON, Samuel	Buckingham	1773	4	
HAMILTON, Samuel	Buckingham	1774	4	
HAMMON, John	Buckingham	1773	3	
HAMMOND, John	Buckingham	1774	3	
HANCOCK, Richard, see Hancock, Solomon				
HANCOCK, Solomon (Tillotson Par.) Hancock, William	Buckingham	1773	5	

Name	County	Year	Tithables	Acres
Hancock, Richard				
HANCOCK, Solomon (Tillotson Par.)	Buckingham	1774	5	
Hancock, William				
Hancock, Richard				
HANCOCK, Thomas (Tillotson Par.)	Buckingham	1773	1	
HANCOCK, William, see Hancock, Solomon				
HANDCOCK, Robt.	Buckingham	1774	1	
HANDCOCK, Thomas	Buckingham	1774	1	
HANDSFORD, Lewis	James City	1768		
HANESFORD, Edward (insolvent)	James City	1768		
HANKIN, Charles	James City	1768	4	270
HANKIN, Charles	James City	1769	4	270
HANKIN, John	James City	1768	4	282
HANKIN, John	James City	1769	4	282
HANKIN, William	James City	1768	6	435
HANKIN, William	James City	1769	7	435
HANNABELL, Phill, see James, Richard				
HANSARD, Archelus	Buckingham	1773	1	
HANSARD, Archer	Buckingham	1774	1	
HANSBROUGH, James	Stafford	1768		262
HANSBROUGH, James	Stafford	1773		262
HANSBROUGH, Morias, see Peters, James				
HANSBROUGH, Morias, of Isaac Savage	Stafford	1768		
HANSBROUGH, Morias, of Savage	Stafford	1773		
HANSBROUGH, Peter, of Fitzhugh	Stafford	1773		340
Do of Burgess Ball				670
HANSBROUGH, Peter	Stafford	1768		131
HANSBROUGH, Peter Sen.	Stafford	1773		131
HANSFORD, John	Buckingham	1773	1	
HANSFORD, Thoms.	James City	1768		
HANSFORD, Thos.*	Gloucester	1770		
HARDEMAN, Baird	Buckingham	1773	1	
HARDEMAN, John	Buckingham	1774	1	
HARDINE, Charles	Stafford	1773		362
"Lost the greatest part of his land by law"				
HARDING, _____, see Hooe, Harris				
HARDING, _____, see Horton, John				
HARDING, Charles	Stafford	1768		362
HARDING, George	Stafford	1768		688
HARDING, Henry	Stafford	1768		644
HARDING, Henry	Stafford	1773		644
HARDING, Supree	Hanover	1763	(1755)	270
HARDWICK, George	Buckingham	1773	2	
Murry, Laurance				
HARDYMAN, John	Buckingham	1773	1	
HARLOW, John	Hanover	1763	(1755)	130
HARMAN, Edward	Buckingham	1773	1	
HARMAN, Edward	Buckingham	1774	1	
HARPER, Ann, see Harper, Edward				
HARPER, Edward and Ann his wife	Gloucester	1770		
HARPER, James (Kingston Parish)	Gloucester	1774	6	
HARPER, James (Kingston Parish)	Gloucester	1775	6	
HARPER, Joseph (St. Martin's Par.)	Hanover	1770	2	
HARRILSON, Burgis	Hanover	1763	(1755)	200
HARIS, John's Quarter	Buckingham	1773	3	
Meglason, William, overseer				
HARRIS, Benjamin	Hanover	1763		714
HARRIS, Daniel	Hanover	1763		191
HARRIS, Daniel, overseer, see James, Richard				
HARRIS, David	Hanover	1763		138

Name	County	Year	Tithables	Acres
HARRIS, Edward	James City	1768	6	195
HARRIS, Edward	James City	1769	5	195
HARRIS, George (a negroe, sic)	Gloucester	1770		
HARRIS, George	Hanover	1763		73
HARRIS, Henry (Kingston Parish)	Gloucester	1774	2	
HARRIS, Henry (Kingston Parish)	Gloucester	1775	2	
HARRIS, James (Kingston Parish)	Gloucester	1774	1	
HARRIS, James (Kingston Parish)	Gloucester	1775	1	
HARRIS, James, see Glover, John Jr.				
HARRIS, John	James City	1769	10	
HARRISS, John (St. Martin's Par.)	Hanover	1770	3	200
HARRIS, John	Hanover	1763	(1762)	120
HARRIS, John	Hanover	1763		36
HARRIS, John	Hanover	1763		200
Do				350
Do				200
HARRIS, John	James City	1768	10	
HARRIS, John	Gloucester	1770	3	
HARRIS, John	Gloucester	1771	4	
HARRIS, John McGlasson, Wm.	Buckingham	1774	4	
HARRIS, John, see Freland, Robt.				
HARRIS, Matthew	Hanover	1763		266
HARRIS, Matthias (Kingston Par.)	Gloucester	1774	2	
HARRIS, Matthias (Kingston Par.)	Gloucester	1775	2	
HARRIS, Overton	Hanover	1763		1380
HARRIS, Peter	Hanover	1763		100
HARRIS, Robert	Hanover	1763		100
HARRIS, Sarah	Hanover	1763		100
Do				62
HARRIS, Sherwood	Hanover	1763		300
HARRIS, Stanley	Hanover	1763		100
HARRIS, Stephen	Hanover	1763		150
HARRIS, Thomas	Hanover	1763		100
HARRIS, Thomas	James City	1768	9	188
HARRIS, Thomas	James City	1769	9	188
HARRIS, William (Creek)	Hanover	1763		400
HARRISS, William St. Martin's Parish	Hanover	1770	4	150
HARRIS, William, see Turpin, Thomas Col.				
HARRISON, Benja., see Bell, Judith				
HARRISON, Benjamin (insolvent)	James City	1768	1	
HARRISON, William	James City	1768	4	50
HARRISON, William	James City	1769	4	50
HARROS (sic), Thomas Kingston Parish	Gloucester	1774	2	
HARROS (sic), Thomas Kingston Parish	Gloucester	1775	2	
HART, John	Hanover	1763		200
HARVEY, Elizabeth	Gloucester	1770		
HARVEY, Elizabeth	Gloucester	1771	3	
HARVY, John	Gloucester	1770	3	
HARVY, John	Gloucester	1771	3	
HARVEY, Thomas	Buckingham	1773	2	
HARVEY, Thomas	Buckingham	1773	1	
HARVEY, Thomas	Buckingham	1774	1	
HARVEY, Thomas Junr.	Buckingham	1774	1	
HARVEY, William	Buckingham	1773	1	
HARVEY, William	Buckingham	1774	2	
HARVY, Wm. Estate	Gloucester	1770	3	150

Name	County	Year	Tithables	Acres
"settled by Eliz. Harvy"				
HARWOOD, John (King & Queen)	Gloucester	1770	5	500
"Quit rent of William Roans"				
HARWOOD, Thos.	Gloucester	1770		
HARWOOD, William	Gloucester	1770	1	
HARWOOD, William	Gloucester	1771	1	
HARWOOD, Wm. Col.	James City	1768		
HATCHER, Archibald	Buckingham	1774	1	
HATCHER, Archibald, see Hobson, John				
HATTEN, Thomas	James City	1768	2	152
HATTEN, Thomas	James City	1769	2	152
HAWKINS, John	Hanover	1763		360
HAWS, William	Hanover	1763		252
HAY, Prisilla	Stafford	1768		75
HAY, Prisilla	Stafford	1773		75
HAY, Thomas	Stafford	1768		350
HAY, Thomas	Stafford	1773		350
HAY, Wm.	Buckingham	1773	1	
HAYES, Hugh (Kingston Parish)	Gloucester	1774	10	
HAYES, Hugh (Kingston Parish)	Gloucester	1775	10	
HAYES, John (Kingston Parish)	Gloucester	1774	13	
HAYES, John (Kingston Parish)	Gloucester	1775	13	
HAYES, Mary (Kingston Parish)	Gloucester	1774	8	
HAYES, Mary (Kingston Parish)	Gloucester	1775	8	
HAYES, Thomas (Kingston Parish)	Gloucester	1774	14	
HAYES, Thomas (Kingston Parish)	Gloucester	1775	14	
HAYNES, James	Gloucester	1770		
HAYWOOD, Cathn., see Vaughan, Edward				
HAYWOOD, Isaac	Gloucester	1770	1	
HAYWOOD, Sarah	Gloucester	1770	3	
HAYWOOD, Sarah	Gloucester	1771	1	
HAZLEWOOD, Benjamin	James City	1768	7	200
HAZLEWOOD, Ben:	James City	1769	4	200
HAZLEWOOD, Dickson	James City	1768	3	250
HAZLEWOOD, Dickson	James City	1769	2	250
HAZLEWOOD, Peggy	James City	1768	4	
HAZLEWOOD, Margret	James City	1769	5	
HAZLEWOOD, Richard	James City	1768	1	
HAZLEWOOD, Richard	James City	1769	1	
HAZLEWOOD, William	Hanover	1763		50
HEART, Elisabeth	James City	1768	3	318
HEDGEMAN, _____, see Knox, John				
HELMS, Exors of, see Pratt, Thomas				
HENCHAN, John, see Murry, Anthony				
HENDCOCK, Benjamin	Hanover	1763		100
HENDERSON, Barbra	Hanover	1763	(1759)	150
HENDERSON, Francis	Gloucester	1770	1	
HENDERSON, Francis	Gloucester	1771	1	
HENDERSON, William	Hanover	1763		100
HENDRICK, William	Hanover	1763		320
HENLEY, Richardson	James City	1768	9	325
HENLEY, Richardson	James City	1769	9	325
HENLEY, Turner	James City	1768	10	680
HENDLEY, Turner	James City	1769	11	680
HENRY, Patrick, the Revd.	Hanover	1763		500
Do				130
HENRY, John	Hanover	1763		630
HENRY, Patrick, Jun.	Hanover	1763		343
HENSLEE, Wm.	Buckingham	1773	1	
HENSLEE, Wm.	Buckingham	1774	1	

Name	County	Year	Tith-ables	Acres
HENSLEE, Zachariah	Buckingham	1773	1	
HENSLEE. Zachariah	Buckingham	1774	1	
HENSLEY, Maxfield	Hanover	1763		150
HESTER, Barbara (St. Martin's Par.)	Hanover	1770	5	431
HESTER, Robert	Hanover	1763	(1761)	866
HEWITT, Richard	Stafford	1768		200
HEWITT, Richard	Stafford	1773		200
HEWLETT, Hannah	James City	1769	3	
HEWS (sic), John	Buckingham	1774	6	
Hughes, Robt.				
HEWS, Ralph	Stafford	1773		800
HEYDON, William Exrs.	Stafford	1768		200
HEYDON, William Exrs.	Stafford	1773		200
HEYWOOD, Abraham	Gloucester	1770	1	
HEYWOOD, Abraham	Gloucester	1771	1	
HEYWOOD, Catharine	Gloucester	1770	5	238
HEYWOOD, Catharine	Gloucester	1771	3	238
HEYWOOD, Elakin (Kingston Parish)	Gloucester	1774	1	
HEYWOOD, Elakin (Kingston Parish)	Gloucester	1775	1	
HEYWOOD, Elizabeth	Gloucester	1770		
HEYWOOD, Jacob*	Gloucester	1770		
HEYWOOD, James	Gloucester	1771	1	
HEYWOOD, Richard	Gloucester	1770	1	
HEYWOOD, Richard	Gloucester	1771		
HEYWOOD, William	Gloucester	1770	3	60
HEYWOOD, William	Gloucester	1771	3	60
HIBBLE, George	Gloucester	1770		
HIBBLE, George	Gloucester	1771	3	
HIBBLE, Treplit (estate)	Gloucester	1770		
HICKMAN, John	James City	1768		
HICKS, Hickerson, see Benning, Joseph				
HICKS, Thomas (St. Martin's Parish)	Hanover	1770	1	
HIGGINSON, Charles	Hanover	1763		200
HIGGINSON, John	Hanover	1763		480
HIGGINSON, Robert	James City	1768	5	
HIGGINSON, Robert	James City	1769	2	
HIGGINSON, Samuel	Hanover	1763		200
HILL, Isaac, see Cabell, John Col.				
HILL. James	Hanover	1763		100
HILL, John	Hanover	1763		150
HILL, Susanna	Hanover	1763		190
HILL, Tho. Mr.	James City	1768		
HILLARD, John, see Adkins, Peter				
(HI)LLIARD, John	Buckingham	1773	1	
HINCHY, John	Hanover	1763		100
HIND, Russell Mr.	Gloucester	1770		400
(John Reade's Est.)				
HINDS, John	Gloucester	1770		
HINES, Caleb	Buckingham	1773	2	
Hines, Thomas				
HINES, Caleb	Buckingham	1774	1	
HINES, Henry, see Johns, John				
HINES, John	Hanover	1763		200
HINES, Thomas	Buckingham	1774	1	
HINES, Thomas, see Hines, Caleb				
HINSON, Benjamin	Hanover	1763	(1760)	156
HINSON, Ch., see Cross, James				
HIX, Henry	Hanover	1763		210
HIX, John	Hanover	1763		222
HIX, William	Hanover	1763		84

Name	County	Year	Tithables	Acres
Do			(1759)	200
HOAR, Elias	Stafford	1768		462
HOBDAY, Frances	Gloucester	1770	1	
HOBDAY, Frances	Gloucester	1771	2	
HOBDAY, Isaac	Gloucester	1770		
"note from York Co. last yr."				
HOBDAY, Isaac	Gloucester	1771	7	
"note from York Co. last yr."				
HOBDAY, John, Chr. Makr.	Gloucester	1770	12	600
(Chair Maker)				
HOBDAY, John, Chr. Makr.	Gloucester	1771	7	600
HOBDAY, John (Pilot)	Gloucester	1770	6	
HOBDAY, John	Gloucester	1771	6	
HOBDAY, Margary	Gloucester	1770	1	50
HOBDAY, Margary (son Richd.)	Gloucester	1771		50
HOBDAY, Richd.	Gloucester	1770	2	
HOBDAY, Richd.	Gloucester	1771	2	
HOBSON, John, at his quarter	Buckingham	1773	5	
Hatcher, Archibald				
HODGES, Benjamin	Buckingham	1773	1	
HODGES, Richd., see Walker, John				
HODGES, Richard (Kingston Parish)	Gloucester	1774	2	
HODGES, Richard (Kingston Parish)	Gloucester	1775	2	
HODNETT, Ayres	Buckingham	1773	3	
HODNETT, John	Buckingham	1773	8	
Hodnett, Phillip				
HODNETT, John	Buckingham	1774	8	
Hodnett, Philop				
HOGG, Fielding	Gloucester	1770	1	
HOGG, Fielding	Gloucester	1771	1	
HOGG, George	Gloucester	1770	2	
HOGG, George	Gloucester	1771	3	
HOGG, George Junr.	Gloucester	1770	1	
HOGG, John	Hanover	1763		50
HOGG, John	Gloucester	1770	1	
HOGG, John	Gloucester	1771	1	
HOGG, Micajah	Hanover	1763		50
HOGG, Milbone	Hanover	1763		50
HOGG, Richd. Jun.	Gloucester	1770	1	
HOGG, Richd. Jun.	Gloucester	1771	1	
HOGG, Richd. Sr.	Gloucester	1770	2	
HOGG, Richd. Sr.	Gloucester	1771	1	
HOGG, Thomas	Hanover	1763		50
HOGGIN, Anne	Hanover	1763		110
HOLDCROFT, James	James City	1768		
HOLDCROFT, William	James City	1768		
HOLDEN, John	Hanover	1763		300
HOLLAND, Michael	Hanover	1763		4606
HOLLIDAY, John	Hanover	1763		240
HOLT, John	James City	1768	3	
HOLT, Margaret	Hanover	1763		1134
HOLT, Matt.	James City	1768	1	
HOLT, William	James City	1768	15	115
HOLT, William	James City	1769	14	115
HOLT, William (Tillotson Parish)	Buckingham	1773	1	
HOPE, John	Hanover	1763		100
HOPKINS, John	Hanover	1763		150
HOOE, Ann	Stafford	1773		623
"Now Wm. Allason's"				
HOOE, Ann Jnr.	Stafford	1768		628

Name	County	Year	Tithables	Acres
HOOE, Ann Senr.	Stafford	1768		998
HOOE, Elias	Stafford	1773		462
HOOE, Gerrard	Stafford	1768		400
HOOE, Gerrard	Stafford	1773		1400
HOOE, Harris of Harding	Stafford	1773		400
HOOE, Howson	Stafford	1768		844
HOOE, Howson	Stafford	1773		844
HOOE, John, see Washington, Nathaniel				
HOOE, Richard Exrs.	Stafford	1768		800
HOOE, Richard Exrs.	Stafford	1774		800
HOOE, Seymour	Stafford	1773		558
HOOE, Susannah	Stafford	1768		628
HOOE, Susannah	Stafford	1773		628
HOOD, Charles	Hanover	1763		123
HOOD, Israel	Hanover	1763		100
HOOD, John	Buckingham	1774	1	
HOOK, Elizabeth	Gloucester	1770		
HOOPER, George	Buckingham	1773	7	
HOOPER, George	Buckingham	1774	7	
HOOPER, James	Hanover	1763		100
HOOPER, Thomas	Hanover	1763		470
HORN, John	Hanover	1763		46
HORNSBY, Thomas	James City	1768	14	332
HORNSBY, Thomas	James City	1769	14	332
HORSELY, Thomas	Gloucester	1770		
HORSELY, Thomas	Gloucester	1771		
HORSLEY, William	Hanover	1763		120
HORTON, H., see Fritter, Moses				
HORTON, Hugh, see Hughs, Ralph				
HORTON, John, of Harding	Stafford	1773		278
HOW, Edward	Gloucester	1770	1 (Ware)	
HOW, Edward	Gloucester	1771		
HOWARD, Benja. Majr. Estate Cobbs, Thomas Bishop, Wm.	Buckingham	1773	23	
HOWARD, Benja. Estate	Buckingham	1774	18	
HOWARD, John	Hanover	1763		1085
HOWARD, Thomas	Gloucester	1770	2	
HOWARD, Thomas	Gloucester	1771	2	
HOWARD, William	Hanover	1763		50
HOWE, James	Buckingham	1773	2	
HOWERTON, Thomas Howerton, James	Buckingham	1774	4	
HOWLETT, Isaac	Gloucester	1770	5	680
HOWLETT, Isaac	Gloucester	1771	8	680
HOWLETT, John	Gloucester	1770	8	449
HOWLETT, John	Gloucester	1771	10	449
HOY, Alexr. (insolvent)	James City	1768		
HOY, John Booker	Buckingham	1773	1	
HOY, William	Buckingham	1774	4	
HOY, Wm. Davison, Edward, overseer	Buckingham	1773	10	
HUBARD, Elizabeth, see Mackentree, Johanna				
HUBARD, James	Gloucester	1770	32	1000
HUBARD, James	Gloucester	1771	26	1000
HUBARD, James, see Hubard, John Capt.				
HUBARD, James Junr.	Gloucester	1770	15	440
HUBARD, James Junr.	Gloucester	1771	15	440
HUBARD, John Capt. (bro. of James)*	Gloucester	1770		
HUBARD, Wm., Capt.	Gloucester	1770		

Name	County	Year	Tith-ables	Acres
HUBARD, Wm., Capt.	Gloucester	1771		
HUCKSTEP, Samuel	Hanover	1763		200
HUDDLESTON, Robert	Buckingham	1773	1	
HUGGLESTON, Robert	Buckingham	1774	1	
HUDGEN, Allin (Kingston Parish)	Gloucester	1774	1	
HUDGEN, Allin (Kingston Parish)	Gloucester	1775	1	
HUDGEN, Gabriel (Kingston Parish)	Gloucester	1774	3	
HUDGEN, Gabriel (Kingston Parish)	Gloucester	1775	3	
HUDGEN, George (Kingston Parish)	Gloucester	1774	2	
HUDGEN, George (Kingston Parish)	Gloucester	1775	2	
HUDGEN, George Junr. Kingston Parish	Gloucester	1774	1	
HUDGEN, George Junr. Kingston Parish	Gloucester	1775	1	
HUDGEN, Humphrey (Kingston Parish)	Gloucester	1774	5	
HUDGEN, Humphrey (Kingston Parish)	Gloucester	1775	5	
HUDGEN, James (Kingston Parish)	Gloucester	1774	1	
HUDGEN, James (Kingston Parish)	Gloucester	1775	1	
HUDGEN, John Senr. (Kingston Par.)	Gloucester	1774	3	
HUDGEN, John Senr. (Kingston Par.)	Gloucester	1775	3	
HUDGEN, Lewis (Kingston Parish)	Gloucester	1774	1	
HUDGEN, Lewis (Kingston Parish)	Gloucester	1775	1	
HUDGEN, Lewis (Kingston Parish)	Gloucester	1774	1	
HUDGEN, Lewis (Kingston Parish)	Gloucester	1775	1	
HUDGEN, Mary (Kingston Parish)	Gloucester	1774	1	
HUDGEN, Mary (Kingston Parish)	Gloucester	1775	1	
HUDGEN, Moses (Kingston Parish)	Gloucester	1774		
HUDGEN, Moses (Kingston Parish)	Gloucester	1775		
HUDGEN, Robert (Kingston Parish)	Gloucester	1774	1	
HUDGEN, Robert (Kingston Parish)	Gloucester	1775	1	
HUDGEN, William (Kingston Parish)	Gloucester	1774	2	
HUDGEN, William (Kingston Parish)	Gloucester	1775	2	
HUDGEN, William (Kingston Parish)	Gloucester	1774	2	
HUDGEN, William (Kingston Parish)	Gloucester	1775	2	
HUDSON, George	Hanover	1763		800
HUDSON, John	Hanover	1763		300
HUDSON, Simon	Buckingham	1773	2	
HUDSON, Simon	Buckingham	1774	2	
HUGGET, Thomas*	Gloucester	1770		
HUGGINS, William	Gloucester	1770	32	701
HUGGINS, William	Gloucester	1771	26	(10 Ware (16 Abingdon
HUGHES, Blackmore	Hanover	1763		117
HUGHES, Edward (Kingston Parish)	Gloucester	1774	10	
HUGHES, Edward (Kingston Parish)	Gloucester	1775	10	
HUGHES, Emery	James City	1769	6	
HUGHES, Gabriel (Kingston Par.)	Gloucester	1774	15	
HUGHES, Gabriel (Kingston Par.)	Gloucester	1775	15	
HUGHES, Henry	Hanover	1763		100
HUGHES, John	Hanover	1763		669
HUGHES, John	Buckingham	1773	1	
HUGHES, John	Buckingham	1774	2	
HUGHES, John, see Hughes, Robt.				
HUGHES, John	Gloucester	1770	12	892
HUGHES, John	Gloucester	1771	15	(3 Petsworth (12 Ware
HUGHES, Rice	Hanover	1763		119
HUGHES, Robt. (Tillotson Par.) Hughes, John	Buckingham	1773	5	
HUGHES, Robt., see Hews, John				

Name	County	Year	Tith-ables	Acres
HUGHES, William	Hanover	1763		379
HUGHES, William Junr.	Hanover	1763		200
Do				200
HUGHS, Emery	James City	1768	3	148½
HUGHS, John, see Hughs, Ralph				
HUGHS, Ralph	Stafford	1768		150
150 Acres of Hugh Horton				
400 Acres of John Hughs				
100 Acres of John Dooling				
HUGHS, Wm., see Combs, John				
HUGHSON, William	Hanover	1763		130
HULETT, Hannah	James City	1768	3	
HUMBER, John	Hanover	1763		50
HUMPHREYS, David	Hanover	1763		200
HUMPHREYS, Edmund	Hanover	1763		100
HUMPHREYS, Edward	Hanover	1763		150
HUMPHREYS, Samuel	Hanover	1763		30
HUNDLY, James	Buckingham	1773	1	
HUNDLY, James	Buckingham	1774	1	
HUNDLY, John	Buckingham	1773	1	
HUNLEY, Ambrose	Hanover	1763		770
HUNLEY, Caleb (Kingston Parish)	Gloucester	1774	1	
HUNLEY, Caleb (Kingston Parish)	Gloucester	1775	1	
HUNLEY, Edward	Hanover	1763		100
Do		(1762)		343
HUNLEY, Henry (Kingston Parish)	Gloucester	1774	1	
HUNLEY, Henry (Kingston Parish)	Gloucester	1775	1	
HUNLEY, Henry (Kingston Parish)	Gloucester	1774	3	
HUNLEY, Henry (Kingston Parish)	Gloucester	1775	3	
HUNLEY, Jacob	Hanover	1763		400
HUNLEY, James (Kingston Parish)	Gloucester	1774	2	
HUNLEY, James (Kingston Parish)	Gloucester	1775	2	
HUNLEY, James (Kingston Parish)	Gloucester	1774	4	
HUNLEY, James (Kingston Parish)	Gloucester	1775	4	
HUNLEY, Jane (Kingston Parish)	Gloucester	1774	1	
HUNLEY, Jane (Kingston Parish)	Gloucester	1775	1	
HUNLEY, John	Hanover	1763		200
HUNLEY, John Senr. (Kingston Par.)	Gloucester	1774	5	
HUNLEY, John Senr. (Kingston Par.)	Gloucester	1775	5	
HUNLEY, Margaret	Hanover	1763		100
HUNLEY, Matthew Senr. Kingston Parish	Gloucester	1774	1	
HUNLEY, Matthew Senr. Kingston Parish	Gloucester	1775	1	
HUNLEY, Richard	Hanover	1763		318½
HUNLEY, Robert (Kingston Par.)	Gloucester	1774	1	
HUNLEY, Robert (Kingston Par.)	Gloucester	1775	1	
HUNLEY, William (Kingston Par.)	Gloucester	1774	1	
HUNLEY, William (Kingston Par.)	Gloucester	1775	1	
HUNT, John	Gloucester	1770	3	100
HUNT, John	Gloucester	1771	2	100
HUNT, John, see Taliaferro, Richard				
HUNTER, John	James City	1768		
HUNTER, James (of James Baxter)	Stafford	1768		1176
HUNTER, James	Stafford	1773		1176
HUNTER, Mary	Gloucester	1770	2	150
HUNTER, Mary	Gloucester	1771	2	150
HURST, Edward (Kingston Par.)	Gloucester	1774	2	
HURST, Edward (Kingston Par.)	Gloucester	1775	2	
HURST, John Exrs.	Stafford	1768		150

Name	County	Year	Tithables	Acres
HURST, John (Kingston Par.)	Gloucester	1774	3	
HURST, John (Kingston Par.)	Gloucester	1775	3	
HURST, Richard (Kingston Par.)	Gloucester	1774	3	
HURST, Richard (Kingston Par.)	Gloucester	1775	3	
HUSE, William (insolvent)	James City	1768	1	
HYLAND, Robert	James City	1768		
INGE, Ambross, see Smith, Thomas				
INGLE, George	Buckingham	1773	1	
INGLE, George	Buckingham	1774	1	
INGRAM, Solomon	Hanover	1763		65
IVERSON, Est., see Whiting, John				
IVERSON, Gregory, see Gregory, Richard				
IVESON, John	Gloucester	1770	2	
IVESON, John	Gloucester	1771	4	
IVESON, Richard	Gloucester	1770	5	134
IVESON, Richard	Gloucester	1771	4	134
IVESON, Robert	Gloucester	1770		
IVESON, Thomas	Gloucester	1770	3	
JACKMAN, William	Gloucester	1770	3	
JACKMAN, William	Gloucester	1771	3	
JACKMAN, William Exrs.	Stafford	1768		239
JACKMAN, William Exrs.	Stafford	1773		239
JAMES, Christopher	Hanover	1763		651
JAMES, Edward	James City	1768	4	
JAMES, Edward	James City	1769	4	
JAMES, George	Stafford	1768		360
JAMES, George	Stafford	1773		360
JAMES, John Elkin	Gloucester	1770	1	
JAMES, John Elkin	Gloucester	1771	1	
JAMES, Matthias (Kingston Par.)	Gloucester	1774	6	
JAMES, Matthias (Kingston Par.)	Gloucester	1775	6	
JAMES, Richard (Tillotson Par.)	Buckingham	1773	11	
Harris, Daniel				
JAMES, Richard	Buckingham	1774	10	
Harris, Daniel, overseer				
Hannabell, Phill				
JAMES, Thruston	James City	1768	9	612
JAMES, Thruston	James City	1769	9	612
JAMES, Walter (Kingston Par.)	Gloucester	1774	3	
JAMES, Walter (Kingston Par.)	Gloucester	1775	3	
JAMISON, Alexr. (of Jno. Saunders)	Stafford	1768		188
JAMISON, Alexr. (of Jno. Saunders)	Stafford	1773		188
JAMISON, Alexander	Stafford	1773		188
JAMISON, Alexander	Stafford	1768		188
JAMISON, David Mr.	James City	1768		
JARRAT, William (Kingston Par.)	Gloucester	1774	1	
JARRAT, William (Kingston Par.)	Gloucester	1775	1	
JARVIS, Francis (Kingston Par.)	Gloucester	1774	1	
JARVIS, Francis (Kingston Par.)	Gloucester	1775	1	
JARVIS, Francis (Kingston Par.)	Gloucester	1774	2	
JARVIS, Francis (Kingston Par.)	Gloucester	1775	2	
JARVIS, Francis, Junr.	Gloucester	1774	1	
Kingston Parish				
JARVIS, Francis, Junr.	Gloucester	1775	1	
Kingston Parish				
JARVIS, John	James City	1768	2	

Name	County	Year	Tithables	Acres
JARVIS, John	James City	1769	3	
JARVIS, John, Senr. Kingston Par.	Gloucester	1774	4	
JARVIS, John, Senr. Kingston Par.	Gloucester	1775	4	
JARVIS, William (Kingston Par.)	Gloucester	1774	2	
JARVIS, William (Kingston Par.)	Gloucester	1775	2	
JEFFERIES, Nathaniel Jefferies, Thomas Jefferies, Nathaniel	Buckingham	1773	5	
JEFFERIES, Nathaniel Jefferies, Thomas Jefferies, Nathaniel	Buckingham	1774	6	
JEFFERSON, Randolph, see Nicholas, John				
JEFFERSON, Randolph Tillotson Parish Bowles, John Slatery, Stephen	Buckingham	1773	13	
JEFFERSON, Randolph	Buckingham	1774	14	
JEFFERYS, John (of Withers)	Stafford	1768		227
JEFFRESS, Joseph, see Smith, Henry Junr.				
JEGITTS, John	James City	1768	6	
JEGITTS, John	James City	1769	6	
JENKINS, Caleb	Gloucester	1770	1	
JENKINS, Caleb	Gloucester	1771	1	
JENKINS, Edward	Buckingham	1773	1	
JENKINS, Edward	Buckingham	1774	1	
JENKINS, James	Gloucester	1770	1	
JENKINS, James	Gloucester	1771	1	
JENKINS, John	Gloucester	1770	1	
JENKINS, John	Gloucester	1771	1	
JENKINS, John	Buckingham	1773	1	
JENKINS, Joseph	Buckingham	1773	1	
JENKINS, Joseph	Buckingham	1773	1	
JENKINS, Obediah	Gloucester	1770	1	
JENKINS, Obediah	Gloucester	1771	1	
JENNINGS, Anderson	Buckingham	1773	1	
JENNINGS, Anderson	Buckingham	1774	1	
JENNINGS, James	James City	1768	3	340
JENNINGS, James	James City	1769	3	340
JENNINGS, James	James City	1768	1	
JENNINGS, James, Jun.	James City	1769	2	
JENNINGS, John	Hanover	1763	81	
JENNINGS, John	Buckingham	1773	1	
JENNINGS, Mary	Hanover	1763		420
Do				75
JENNINGS, Moody	Hanover	1763		450
JENNINGS, Robert	Hanover	1763		119
JENNINGS, William	Buckingham	1773	1	
JENNINGS, William	Buckingham	1774	1	
JENNINGS, William, see Pryer, Sarah				
JERDONE, Francis (St. Martin's Par.)	Hanover	1770	30	1188
JEWELL, (Thomas), bot (sic) of Cook	Stafford	1768		450
JEWELL, Thomas	Stafford	1773		450
JINNINGS, John	Buckingham	1774	1	
JOHNS, James	Buckingham	1774	1	
JOHNS, Jesse	Buckingham	1773	5	
JOHNS, Jesse Garnett, Edwin	Buckingham	1774	6	
JOHNS, John	Buckingham	1773	1	

Name	County	Year	Tithables	Acres
JOHNS, John:	Buckingham	1773	8	
Hines, Henry				
JOHNS, John	Buckingham	1774	8	
Richardson, Stanup				
Moss, John				
JOHNS, Josiah	Buckingham	1773	1	
JOHNS, Josiah	Buckingham	1774	2	
JOHNS, Mallory (mulatto)	Buckingham	1773	1	
Tillotson Parish				
JOHNS, Salley	Buckingham	1773	1	
JOHNS, Thomas	Buckingham	1773	3	
JOHNS, Thomas	Buckingham	1774	3	
JOHNS, William	Buckingham	1773	2	
JOHNS, William	Buckingham	1774	4	
Wood, Thos.				
JOHNS, William Jr.	Buckingham	1773	2	
JOHNS, Wm. Junr.	Buckingham	1774	4	
Day, Ambrose				
JOHNSON, Benjamin	Hanover	1763		200
JOHNSON, David	Hanover	1763		200
JOHNSON, George (St. Martin's Par.)	Hanover	1770	6	151
JOHNSON, James Bray (insolvent)	James City	1768		
JOHNSON, Josiah Revd.	James City	1769	2	
JOHNSON, Nicholas	Hanover	1763		(1759) 175
JOHNSON, Phil. Coll.	James City	1768	23	4125
		also	40	
JOHNSON, Phillip	James City	1769	40	4125
"to 43 Tithes"				
JOHNSON, Richd., see Gannaway, John Jr.				
JOHNSON, Richd. Col.	James City	1768		
JOHNSON, Samuel	Gloucester	1770	1	
JOHNSON, Samuel	Gloucester	1771		
JOHNSON, Thomas	Hanover	1763		178
JOHNSON, Thos.*	Gloucester	1770		
JOHNSON, William	Hanover	1763		190)
Do				200)
JOHNSON, William (St.Martin's Par.)	Hanover	1770		
JOHNSON, Wm.	Buckingham	1774	1	
JOHNSON, Wm., see Cabell, Col. Joseph				
JOHNSTON, George	Gloucester	1770	3	
"To Clerk's note Middlesex"				
JOHNSTON, John (Kingston Parish)	Gloucester	1774	2	
JOHNSTON, John (Kingston Parish)	Gloucester	1775	2	
JOHNSTON, John, see Nicholas, John				
JOINER, William	Hanover	1763		400
JONES, see Gist, Samuel				
JONES, Abraham	Buckingham	1774	1	
JONES, Allen	James City	1769		
JONES, Ann	Gloucester	1770		270
JONES, Ann	Gloucester	1771		270
JONES, Calvert	Stafford	1768		109
JONES, Calvert	Stafford	1773		109
JONES, Charles	Hanover	1763		247
JONES, Charles Estate	Gloucester	1774	3	
Kingston Parish				
JONES, Charles Estate	Gloucester	1775	3	
Kingston Parish				
JONES, Daniel	Buckingham	1773	5	
JONES, Daniel	Buckingham	1774	4	
JONES, Elias	Buckingham	1773	1	

Name	County	Year	Tithables	Acres
JONES, Elias	Buckingham	1774	2	
JONES, Emanuel	James City	1768		
JONES, George	Hanover	1763		80
JONES, Isaac (Kingston Parish)	Gloucester	1774		
JONES, Isaac (Kingston Parish)	Gloucester	1775		
JONES, James	James City	1768	1	100
JONES, James	James City	1769	2	100
JONES, James	James City	1768	3	
JONES, James	James City	1769	3	
JONES, James	Gloucester	1770		
JONES, James (Kingston Parish)	Gloucester	1774	4	
JONES, James (Kingston Parish)	Gloucester	1775	4	
JONES, Jno., see Willis, Mesheck				
JONES, John	James City	1768		
JONES, John	James City	1768	1	55
JONES, John	James City	1769	1	55
JONES, John	James City	1768	2	100
JONES, John	James City	1769	2	100
JONES, John	Hanover	1763		350
Do				333
Do				112
JONES, John	Gloucester	1770	5	
JONES, John	Gloucester	1771	6	
JONES, John	Buckingham	1773	10	
Jones, John Jr.				
Jones, Thomas				
JONES, John	Buckingham	1774	9	
Burton, Wm.				
Jones, Thomas				
JONES, Joseph	James City	1768	3	
JONES, Joseph	James City	1769	4	
JONES, Joshua	James City	1768	1	
JONES, Joshua	James City	1769	2	
JONES, Josiah	Buckingham	1773	5	
Williams, John				
JONES, Josiah	Buckingham	1774	6	
Smith, Robert				
JONES, Mary	James City	1768	7	117
JONES, Mary	James City	1769	5	117
JONES, Nelson	Gloucester	1770		
JONES, Peter, see Lambath, William				
JONES, Richard	Hanover	1763		100
JONES, Richard	Gloucester	1770	25	1200
JONES, Richard	Gloucester	1771	27	1200
JONES, Robert	Buckingham	1773	3	
JONES, Robert	Buckingham	1774	3	
JONES, Rowland	Hanover	1763		310
JONES, Samuel	James City	1768		
JONES, Stephen	James City	1769	2	
JONES, Thomas	Hanover	1763		200
JONES, Thomas (Kingston Parish)	Gloucester	1774	3	
JONES, Thomas (Kingston Parish)	Gloucester	1775	3	
JONES, Thomas, see Jones, John				
JONES, William	Hanover	1763		200
JONES, William	James City	1768	2	100
JONES, William	James City	1769	2	100
JONES, William	James City	1768	2	
JONES, William	James City	1769	2	
JONES, William	Gloucester	1770	4	230
JONES, William	Gloucester	1771		230

Name	County	Year	Tithables	Acres
JONES, William (Tillotson Par.)	Buckingham	1773	6	
JONES, William (Tillotson Par.)	Buckingham	1774	7	
JONES, Wm.	James City	1768	2	100
JONES, Wm., see Jordan, Samuel				
JONES, William (Cumberland)	Hanover	1763		160
JORDAIN, John M.	James City	1768		
JORDAN, Reubin, "at his Quarter" Hamblet, Archer	Buckingham	1773	5	
JORDAN, Reuben (Tillotson Par.) Hamblet, Archer	Buckingham	1773	6	
JORDAN, Robert	James City	1769	3	283
JORDAN, Samuel Jones, Wm.	Buckingham	1773	13	
JORDON, Samuel Goolsby, Daniel	Buckingham	1774	13	
JORDAN, Thomas*	Gloucester	1770		
KAMMEL, John	Gloucester	1770	1	
KAMMEL, John	Gloucester	1771	1	
KEELING, G., see Ramsey, Benjamin				
KEELING, George	James City	1768		
KEEN, Mary	James City	1768	3	168
KEEN, Mary	James City	1769	3	168
KEETON, John	Gloucester	1770	2	
KEETON, John	Gloucester	1771	2	
KEININGHAM, Benjamin	Gloucester	1770	2	
KEININGHAM, Benjamin	Gloucester	1771	2	
KEININGHAM, Elizabeth	Gloucester	1770	5	100
KEININGHAM, Elizabeth	Gloucester	1771	5	100
KEININGHAM, Jane	Gloucester	1770	2	
KEININGHAM, Jane	Gloucester	1771	2	
KEININGHAM, John	Gloucester	1770	1	100
KEININGHAM, John	Gloucester	1771	2	100
KEININGHAM, William	Gloucester	1770	1	100
KEININGHAM, William	Gloucester	1771	1	100
KELLY, Wilford	Stafford	1768		50
KELLEY, Wilford	Stafford	1773		50
KEMP, Peter	Gloucester	1770	13	831
KEMP, Peter	Gloucester	1771	14	831
KEMP, Robert	Gloucester	1770		
KEMP, Thomas	Gloucester	1770	4	300
KEMP, Thomas	Gloucester	1771	3	130
KEMP, Wm.*	Gloucester	1770		
KEMP, Wm.*	Gloucester	1771		
KEMP, William Junr.	Gloucester	1770	4	290
KEMP, William Junr.	Gloucester	1771	4	290
KENDALL, John	Stafford	1773		600
KENDALL, Joshua	Stafford	1768		146
KENDALL, Joshua	Stafford	1773		146
KENDALL, William	Stafford	1773		196
KENNADAY, Charles	Hanover	1763		400
KENNY, James	Stafford	1768		163
KENNEY, James	Stafford	1773		163
KENNEY, Jas., see Cason, Thomas				
KENNON, Wm. Col.	Gloucester	1770		
KENP, William	Hanover	1763		120
KENT, Abraham	Hanover	1763		75
KENT, Robert	Hanover	1763		100
KERR, Andrew (Kingston Parish)	Gloucester	1774	3	

Name	County	Year	Tithables	Acres
KERR, Andrew (Kingston Parish)	Gloucester	1775	3	
KERR, George	James City	1768		
KERSEY, Alexander	Hanover	1763		(1759)100
KERSEY, Edward (Tillotson Par.)	Buckingham	1773	2	
Kersey, Edwd. Jun.				
KEYES, Edward (Kingston Parish)	Gloucester	1774	1	
KEYES, Edward (Kingston Parish)	Gloucester	1775	1	
KEYES, Robert (Kingston Parish)	Gloucester	1774	2	
KEYES, Robert (Kingston Parish)	Gloucester	1775	2	
KEYS, John	Gloucester	1770		
KIDD, Benjamin	Buckingham	1773	1	
KIDD, James	Buckingham	1773	1	
KIDD, John (Tillotson Parish)	Buckingham	1773	1	
KIDD, John (Tillotson Parish)	Buckingham	1774	1	
KIDD, Lewis overseer, see Cobbs, John				
KIDD, Moses	Buckingham	1773	1	
KIDD, Moses	Buckingham	1774	1	
KIDD, Samuel	Buckingham	1773	1	
KIDD, Samuel	Buckingham	1774	1	
KIDD, Wm.	Buckingham	1774	1	
KIDD, Wm., see Allen, George Hunt				
KIMBROW, Major	Hanover	1763		125
KINDSMAN, Allen (sic), see Allen, John				
KING, ____ (His Quarters)	Buckingham	1773	21	
Bush, John				
Page, Robert				
KING, Ann (Kingston Parish)	Gloucester	1774		
KING, Ann (Kingston Parish)	Gloucester	1775		
KING, Ann, widow (Kingston Par.)	Gloucester	1774		
KING, Ann, widow (Kingston Par.)	Gloucester	1775		
KING, Elisabeth	Stafford	1768		280
Do		of William George		161
Do		of Isaac Bridwell		72
KING, Elisabeth	Stafford	1773		613
KING, John	Hanover	1768		130
KING, John (Kingston Parish)	Gloucester	1774	4	
KING, John (Kingston Parish)	Gloucester	1775	4	
KING, Joseph (Kingston Parish)	Gloucester	1774	4	
KING, Joseph (Kingston Parish)	Gloucester	1775	4	
KING, Rachel	Hanover	1763		190
KING, Thomas	Hanover	1763	(1762)	330
KING, Thomas (Kingston Parish)	Gloucester	1774	2	
KING, Thomas (Kingston Parish)	Gloucester	1775	2	
KING, Walter Mr.	Buckingham	1774	25	
Boaze, Robt.				
Bush, John				
KING, Withers, see Bridewell, Abraham				
KIRBY, Henry	Hanover	1763		50
KIRBY, Henry, Jun.	Hanover	1763		100
KIRBY, William	Hanover	1763		75
Do				219
KITCHEN, Anthony	Stafford	1768		150
KITCHEN, Bohannah	Buckingham	1774	1	
KITCHEN, Buchanon	Buckingham	1773	1	
KITCHIN, Anthony, see Gray, George				
KNIGHT, Henry (Kingston Parish)	Gloucester	1774	5	
KNIGHT, Henry (Kingston Parish)	Gloucester	1775	5	
KNOT, William	Gloucester	1771	1	
KNOX, John	Stafford	1768	of Whitley	266

Name	County	Year	Tithables	Acres
Do		of Williams		71
Do		of Hedgeman		7189
KNOX, John (of William)	Stafford	1773		71
Do		of Whitley		266
Do		of Hedgeman		789
KNOX, Robt., see Ralls, John				
KNOX, Wm., see Knox, John				
KYLE, Robert	Buckingham	1773	5	
Kyle, David				
KYLE, Robt.	Buckingham	1774	5	
Kyle, David				
Kyle, Robt.				
LACEY, John	James City	1768		
LACEY, Stephen	Hanover	1763		170
LAINE, Wm. Sealy	James City	1768		
LAMB, Mary	Gloucester	1770		50
LAMBATH, William	Buckingham	1773	3	
Jones, Peter				
Meggison, Benja.				
LANDERS, Robt.	Buckingham	1774	1	
LANE, Daniel	Gloucester	1770		150
LANE, Daniel	Gloucester	1771	1	150
LANGHORN, Morris	Buckingham	1773	9	
Furlong, Robert				
LANGSDEN, John	Hanover	1763		100
LANKFORD, Edward	Hanover	1763		432
LANKFORD, Hiram	Gloucester	1770		
LARK, Jonathan	James City	1768	1	
LARK, Jonathan	James City	1769	1	
LARK(E), Robert	James City	1768	1	100
LARK(E), Robert	James City	1769	2	100
LAUGHLIN, Francis	Gloucester	1770	1	
LAUGHLIN, Francis	Gloucester	1771		
LAUGHLIN, James*	Gloucester	1770		
LAUGHLIN, Simon	Gloucester	1770		
LAUGHLIN, Thomas (Middlesex)	Gloucester	1770		180
LAWRENCE, Balden &c	James City	1768		
LAWS &c	James City	1768		
LAWRENCE, John	Hanover	1763		280
LAWSON, John	Gloucester	1770	3	
LAWSON, John	Gloucester	1771	4	
LAX, James	Buckingham	1773	1	
LAX, James	Buckingham	1774	1	
LAYN, Charles	Buckingham	1773	2	
Layn, Jesse				
LAYNE, Charles	Buckingham	1774	1	
LAYNE, Jesse	Buckingham	1774	1	
LEAVET, Thomas*	Gloucester	1770		
LEAVIT, Edmund	Gloucester	1770	4	394
LEAVIT, Edmund	Gloucester	1771	5	394
LEAVIT, Susanna	Gloucester	1770		50
LEAVIT, Susanna	Gloucester	1771		50
LEAVIT, William*	Gloucester	1770		
LEE, Archibald, see Lee, Richd.				
LEE, Arthur	James City	1768	3	
LEE, Evan	Buckingham	1773	2	
Neel, Wm.				
LEE, Evan	Buckingham	1774	1	

Name	County	Year	Tithables	Acres
LEE, Francis (Estate)	Gloucester	1770		1130
LEE, Francis (Estate)	Gloucester	1771		1130
LEE, Gresham Franklin, Hen.	Buckingham	1773	2	
LEE, John	Buckingham	1773	1	
LEE, Lud. Thomas	Stafford	1768	In Stafford	1127
Do			In Loudoun	4481
Do			In Fairfax	5830
Do			In Fauquier	2945
LEE, Ludwell Thos.	Stafford	1773	In Stafford	1227
Do			In Loudoun	4481
Do			In Fairfax	5830
Do			In Fauquier	2945
LEE, Richard	Buckingham	1773	1	
LEE, Richd. Lee, Archibald	Buckingham	1774	2	
LEE, Robert	Hanover	1763		130
LEE, Wm., see Pattison, Thos.				
LEE, Young	Buckingham	1773	1	
LEGAN, John, see Thomas, Henry				
LEITH, Sarah*	Gloucester	1770		
LEMAY, Charles	Hanover	1763		510
LEMMON, Ambrose	Gloucester	1770	3	
LEMMON, Ambrose	Gloucester	1771	3	
LEMMON, James	Gloucester	1770	1	
LEMMON, James	Gloucester	1771	1	
LEMMON, Joshua	Gloucester	1770	1	
LEMMON, Richard	Gloucester	1770	2	
LEMMON, Richard Junr.	Gloucester	1770	1	
LEMMON, Robert	Gloucester	1770		
LEMMON, William	Gloucester	1770		
LEMMON, William Junr.	Gloucester	1770	1	
LESEURE, Samuel	Buckingham	1774	2	
LESURE, Chastain	Buckingham	1774	2	
LESURE, James	Buckingham	1774	3	
LESURE, Samuel	Buckingham	1773	2	
LEWELLEN, Christopher	Gloucester	1770	1	
LEWELLEN, Christopher	Gloucester	1771	2	
LEWIS, Christopher Kingston Parish	Gloucester	1774	1	
LEWIS, Christopher Kingston Parish	Gloucester	1775	1	
LEWIS, Henry	Gloucester	1770		
LEWIS, Jacob	James City	1768		
LEWIS, John	James City	1768		
LEWIS, John	James City	1769	4	557
LEWIS, John	Gloucester	1770		
LEWIS, John	Gloucester	1771		
LEWIS, John Junr.	Gloucester	1770		
LEWIS, John Junr.	Gloucester	1771		
LEWIS, John	Hanover	1763		240
LEWIS, Lucretia (Kingston Par.)	Gloucester	1774	2	
LEWIS, Lucretia (Kingston Par.)	Gloucester	1775	2	
LEWIS, Nicholas*	Gloucester	1770		
LEWIS, Owin, see Tindal, Benjamin				
LEWIS, Oleun, overseer, see Tindall, Benjamin				
LEWIS, Robert (Kingston Par.)	Gloucester	1774	1	
LEWIS, Robert (Kingston Par.)	Gloucester	1775	1	

Name	County	Year	Tithables	Acres
LEWIS, Thomas*	Gloucester	1770		
LEWIS, Warner*	Gloucester	1770		
LEWIS, Warner Capt.	Gloucester	1770		
LEWIS, Warner Capt.	Gloucester	1771	12	Ware
Do			18	Abingdon
LEWIS, Warner Jr., Lt. Cn.	Gloucester	1770	14	Ware
LEWIS, Warner Jr., Lt. Cn.	Gloucester	1771	12	Ware
LEWIS, William	James City	1768	3	64
LEWIS, William	James City	1768	3	
LEWIS, Wm.	James City	1769	1	
LEWIS, William	James City	1769	1	
LEWIS, Wm. James	James City	1769	2	64
LIGGON, Elijah	Hanover	1763		100
LIGHTFOOT, John	James City	1768	6	300
LIGHTFOOT, Phil., Estate	James City	1768		
LIGHTFOOT, Sherwood	James City	1768		
LIGON, Jno., see Agee, Matthew				
LILLY, William (Kingston Par.)	Gloucester	1774	12	
LILLY, William (Kingston Par.)	Gloucester	1775	12	
LINDSAY, Jeremiah	Hanover	1763		231
LINSEY, Elisabeth	James City	1768	3	170
LINSEY, Richard	James City	1768	1	50
LINSEY, Richard	James City	1769	1	50
LINSEY, Elizabeth	James City	1769	2	170
LIPSCOMB, Moses	Hanover	1763		700
LIPSCOMBE, Thomas (St. Martin's)	Hanover	1770	12	180
LITTLE, John (Kingston Parish)	Gloucester	1774	2	
LITTLE, John (Kingston Parish)	Gloucester	1775	2	
LITTLEPAGE, James	Hanover	1763		3842
LIVELY, Edward	Hanover	1763		100
LIVINGSTON, Cornelius*	Gloucester	1770		
Est. of Brother George				
LIVINGSTON, George	Gloucester			
LIVINGSTON, George Est., see Livingston, Cornelius				
LIVINGSTON, Mary	Gloucester	1770		
LOCKET, David	Buckingham	1773	5	
LOCKET, David	Buckingham	1774	5	
LONGEST, Ann (Kingston Parish)	Gloucester	1774		
LONGEST, Ann (Kingston Parish)	Gloucester	1775		
LONGEST, Mildred	Gloucester	1770		
LONGEST, Thomas (Kingston Parish)	Gloucester	1774	1	
LONGEST, Thomas (Kingston Parish)	Gloucester	1775	1	
LOW, Alexander	Buckingham	1773	1	
LOW, Daniel Johnson	Buckingham	1773	6	
Low, Daniel				
LOW, Daniel Johnson	Buckingham	1774	6	
Low, Daniel				
LOW, Jesse	Buckingham	1774	1	
LOW, Wm.	Buckingham	1773	7	
Rutherford, Larkin				
LOW, William	Buckingham	1774	7	
Williams, John				
LOWERY, Mary (Kingston Par.)	Gloucester	1774	1	
LOWERY, Mary (Kingston Par.)	Gloucester	1775	1	
LUCAS, George	Hanover	1763		100
LUCAS, William (Kingston Par.)	Gloucester	1774		
LUCAS, William (Kingston Par.)	Gloucester	1775		
LUCAS, William (Kingston Par.)	Gloucester	1774	5	
LUCAS, William (Kingston Par.)	Gloucester	1775	5	
LUCK, John	Hanover	1763		212

Name	County	Year	Tithables	Acres
LUCK, John Junr.	Hanover	1763		100
LUCK, Samuel	Hanover	1763		125
LUDWELL, Phillip Esqr. Est.	James City	1768	14	8937
also 126 Tithes James City Parish				
LUDWELL, Phillip, Est.	James City	1769	13	8937
"to 128 tithes"				
LUKER, John	James City	1768		
LUMSDEN, Georg (St. Martin's)	Hanover	1770	3	50
LUNSFORD, Moses	Stafford	1773		100
LUTTRELL, _____, see Colson, Charles				
LYELL, Jonathan	Gloucester	1770	3	390
LYELL, Jonathan	Gloucester	1771	4	390
LYNE, John	Gloucester	1770		
LYNE, John	Gloucester	1771		
LYNN, John (of Jos. Smith)	Stafford	1773		133
LYON, John	James City	1768	3	100
LYON, John	James City	1769	3	100
LYON, Robert	James City	1768		
LYONS, Peter	Hanover	1763		435
MACHEN, John (Kingston Par.)	Gloucester	1774	6	
MACHEN, John (Kingston Par.)	Gloucester	1775	6	
MACHEN, Judith (Kingston Par.)	Gloucester	1774		
MACHEN, Judith (Kingston Par.)	Gloucester	1775		
MACHEN, Robert (Kingston Par.)	Gloucester	1774	1	
MACHEN, Robert (Kingston Par.)	Gloucester	1775	1	
MACHEN, Samuel (Kingston Par.)	Gloucester	1774	1	
MACHEN, Samuel (Kingston Par.)	Gloucester	1775	1	
MACKASHANE, Richard	Buckingham	1773	1	
MACKENTREE, Johanna	Gloucester	1770		170
Elizabeth Hubard owns ½ the land				
MACK WILLIAMS, Thomas	Gloucester	1770		
MACMANAWY, John	Buckingham	1774	1	
MACON, William	Hanover	1763		600
MACON, William Junr.	Hanover	1763		1200
MACRAE, Christopher, see Urquhart, Walter				
MADDISON, Farquhar	Hanover	1763	(1759)	446
MADDOX, Jacob	Buckingham	1773	1	
MADDOX, Jacob	Buckingham	1774	1	
MADDOX, Stephen, see Maddox, Wm.				
MADDOX, Wm.	Buckingham	1773	5	
Maddox, Stephen				
MADDOX, Wm.	Buckingham	1774	5	
Maddox, Stephen				
MAHONE, Major	James City	1768	2	
MAHONE, Major	James City	1769	2	
MALCOM, James	Buckingham	1773	1	
MALIUM, James, see Stinson, David				
MALOID, David	Buckingham	1773	4	
Blackburn, John				
MALLOID, David	Buckingham	1774	4	
MALLORY, Charles	Hanover	1763		109
MALLORY, Sarah	Hanover	1763		100
MALLORY, Thomas	Hanover	1763		456
MALLORY, William	Hanover	1763		115
MANN, Thomas	Stafford	1768		274
MANN, Thomas	Stafford	1774		274
MANNIN, William	Buckingham	1773	1	
MANNING, Samuel	Buckingham	1774	1	

Name	County	Year	Tithables	Acres
MANNYS, Henry	Gloucester	1771	2	
MANSFIELD, John	Hanover	1763		725
MARCH, John	Gloucester	1770		
MARCH, Richard	Gloucester	1770	3	112
MARCH, Richard	Gloucester	1771	3	112
MARCH, Thomas	Gloucester	1770	3	
MARCH, Thomas	Gloucester	1771	3	
MARCHANT, Ambrose (Kingston Par.)	Gloucester	1774	6	
MARCHANT, Ambrose (Kingston Par.)	Gloucester	1775	6	
MARCHANT, Edmond (Kingston Par.)	Gloucester	1774	1	
MARCHANT, Edmond (Kingston Par.)	Gloucester	1775	1	
MARCHANT, Elisha (Kingston Par.)	Gloucester	1774	4	
MARCHANT, Elisha (Kingston Par.)	Gloucester	1775	4	
MARCHANT, Richard (Kingston Par.)	Gloucester	1774	2	
MARCHANT, Richard (Kingston Par.)	Gloucester	1775	2	
MARCHANT, William Junr. Kingston Parish	Gloucester	1774	1	
MARCHANT, William Junr. Kingston Parish	Gloucester	1775	1	
MARKHAM, James, see Savage, William				
MARKS, Peter	Hanover	1763		570
MARNIX, Isaac	Gloucester	1770	1	
MARNIX, Isaac	Gloucester	1771	1	
MARNIX, John	Gloucester	1770	1	
MARNIX, John	Gloucester	1771	1	
MARNIX, Thomas	Gloucester	1770	1	
MARNIX, Thomas	Gloucester	1771	1	
MARSHALL, John (St. Martin's)	Hanover	1770	3	130
MARTER, Jonkin (insolvent)	James City	1768	1	
MARTIN, Barbra	Hanover	1763		150
MARTIN, George, see Bristow, James				
MARTIN, Jeremiah	James City	1768	4	37
MARTIN, Jeremiah	James City	1769	5	37
MARTIN, John	Jemes City	1768		
MARTIN, John Martin, James Martin, John	Buckingham	1773	3	
MARTIN, Wm.	Buckingham	1773	2	
MARTIN, Wm., Junr.	Buckingham	1774	2	
MARTIN, Wm., Senr.	Buckingham	1773	1	
MARTIN, Wm., Senr.	Buckingham	1774	1	
MARQUES, Jno. (of Grigsby)	Stafford	1773		90
MASE, Silvanus, Ferry Keeper	Buckingham	1773	1	
MASK, John	Hanover	1763		100
MASK, William	Hanover	1763		208
MASON, John	Stafford	1768		100
MASON, John	Stafford	1773		100
MASON, Peleg	Gloucester	1770	1	
MASON, Peleg	Gloucester	1771	2	
MASON, Peter	Hanover	1763		100
MASON, Thomas	Gloucester	1770		
MASON, Tomson	Stafford	1768 Stafford		1800
Do		P. William		770
Do		Loudoun		3336
Do	For Saml. Selden, Junr.			4016
MASON, William	Stafford	1768		100
MASON, William	Stafford	1773		100
MASSEY, Charles	Stafford	1768		708
MASSEY, Charles	Stafford	1773		508

Name	County	Year	Tithables	Acres
MASSEY, Charles, see Dade, Codwallader, Junt.				
MASSEY, Robert Mr.	Gloucester	1771	10	
Blassingane, John Q.R.				
Mrs. Yates Q.R.				
MASSEY, Segismond	Stafford	1773		420
MASSEY, Segivimd (sic)	Stafford	1768		420
MASSEY, Thomas	Stafford	1768		400
MASSEY, Thomas	Stafford	1773		400
Do	of Gerrard Fowke			300
MASSEY, William, see Yates, Mary				
MASSIE, James	Hanover	1763		200
MASSIE, Peter	James City	1768		
MASSIE, Peter	James City	1768		
MASSIE, Silvanus	Buckingham	1774	1	
MASSIE, William	Hanover	1763		300
MASTERS, James	Buckingham	1774	1	
MASTERS, John	Buckingham	1774	3	
Masters, Wm.				
Masters, John				
MATHEWS, Thomas	Buckingham	1773	2	
MATHEWS, William	Stafford	1768		200
MATTHEWS, Francis	James City	1769	2	
MATTHEWS, Gregory	Buckingham	1773	7	
MATTHEWS, Gregory	Buckingham	1774	4	
MATTHEWS, James	Hanover	1763		132
MATTHEWS, James	Buckingham	1773	4	
Matthews, Joel				
MATTHEWS, James	Buckingham	1774	4	
Matthews, Joel				
MATTHEWS, John	Hanover	1763		133
MATTHEWS, John Estate	Gloucester	1774	6	
Kingston Parish				
MATTHEWS, John Estate	Gloucester	1775	6	
Kingston Parish				
MATTHEWS, Moses	Gloucester	1771	2	
MATTHEWS, Richard (Kingston Par.)	Gloucester	1774		
MATTHESS, Richard (Kingston Par.)	Gloucester	1775		
MATTHEWS, Robert (Kingston Par.)	Gloucester	1774	15	
MTTTHEWS, Robert (Kingston Par.)	Gloucester	1775	15	
MATTHEWS, Samuel	Buckingham	1774	1	
MATTHEWS, Thos.	Buckingham	1774	3	
MATLOCK, Charles	Hanover	1763	(1756)	298
MATLOCK, George	Hanover	1763		92
MATLOCK, Stephen	Hanover	1763	(1755)	190
MAUPIN, Gabriel	James City	1768	9	360
MAUPIN, Gabriel	James City	1769	13	360
MAUZY, John Jr.	Stafford	1768		305
MAUZY, John Jr.	Stafford	1773		305
MAUZY, John Senr.	Stafford	1768		109
MAUZY, John Senr.	Stafford	1773		109
MAXEY, Charles	Buckingham	1774	2	
MAXEY, Edward	Buckingham	1773	2	
Maxey, John				
MAXEY, Edward	Buckingham	1774	2	
Maxey, John				
MAXEY, Nathaniel	Buckingham	1773	1	
MAXEY, Nathaniel	Buckingham	1774	1	
MAXEY, Sampson	Buckingham	1773	1	
MAXEY, Samson	Buckingham	1774	1	
MAY, Chas.	Buckingham	1773	5	

Name	County	Year	Tithables	Acres
MAY, Charles	Buckingham	1774	7	
May, John				
MAY, John	Hanover	1763		150
MAY, John	Buckingham	1773	1	
MAY, John	Buckingham	1774	1	
MAY, John, see May, Charles				
MAY, Nicholas	Hanover	1763		100
MAYO, Thos., see Cobbs, Thos.				
MAYO, Valentine	Buckingham	1773	2	
MAYO, Valentine	Buckingham	1774	2	
MAYS, John (Tillotson Parish)	Buckingham	1773	1	
McCALLUM, Danl., see Nicholas, John				
McCORMACK,	Buckingham	1774	1	
McCORMACK, David	Buckingham	1773	1	
McCORMACK, David, see McCormack, Thomas				
McCORMACK, Hugh	Buckingham	1773	1	
McCORMACK, John	Buckingham	1773	1	
McCORMACK, John	Buckingham	1774	1	
McCORMACK, Sheerwood	Buckingham	1773	1	
McCORMACK, Thomas	Buckingham	1773	2	
McCormack, David, his son				
McCORMACK, Thomas	Buckingham	1774	2	
McCormack, David, his son				
McCORMIT, John	Stafford	1768		100
McCORMIT, John	Stafford	1773		100
McDOWELL, James	James City	1768	6	900
McDOWELL, James	James City	1769	6	900
McENTIRE, Alexander	Stafford	1773		200
McFADEEN, Farrel	Buckingham	1773	1	
McGEORGE, John	Hanover	1763		425
McGHEE, John	Hanover	1763		131
McGHEE, John (St. Martin's)	Hanover	1770	8	400
McGHEE, Samuel	Hanover	1763	(1756)	100
McGHEE, Samuel (St. Martin's)	Hanover	1770	11	400
NcGHEE, William (St. Martin's)	Hanover	1770	8	306
McGLASSON, James, see McGlasson, Wm.				
McGLASSON, Matthew	Buckingham	1774	1	
McGLASSON, Wm.	Buckingham	1774	3	
McGlasson, James				
McGLASSON, Wm., see Harris, John				
McLAUGHLAND, George	Hanover	1763	(1759)	100
McLOUD, John, see Bolling, Archibald				
McNAMARAH, William	Hanover	1763		147
McSHANE, Nehemiah	Buckingham	1773	4	
McSHANE, Nehemiah	Buckingham	1774	5	
McSHANE, Richard	Buckingham	1774	1	
McTIRE, Rachel	James City	1769	1	
MEAD, John	Hanover	1763		600
MEANLEY, William	Buckingham	1773	1	
MECKINS, Mary	James City	1768		
MECOSKRY, Samuel	Gloucester	1770		
MECOSKRY, Samuel	Gloucester	1771		
MEDLICOT, George	Gloucester	1770	1	
MEDLICOT, George	Gloucester	1771	1	
MEDLOCK, Nathaniel	Buckingham	1773	1	
MEDLOCK, Nathaniel	Buckingham	1774	1	
MEEKE (or MEEKIE), John	Hanover	1763		235
MEGARY, Thomas (insolvent)	James City	1768	1	
MEGGISON, Benja., see Lambeth, William				
MEGGS, Joel, see Cannon, William				

Name	County	Year	Tithables	Acres
MEGLASON, William	Buckingham	1773	3	
Meglason, James				
Meglason, Matthew				
MEGLASON, William, see Haris, John				
MEHITTRICK, Robert	James City	1768		
MELTON, Joel	Hanover	1763		90
MELTON, Mary	Hanover	1763		33
MERCER, George	Stafford	1768		145
Do (for deeds in his own name)				1117
MERCER, George Sen.	Stafford	1773		145
Do (Deed in his own name)				1117
MERCER, George & James	Stafford	1768		16,197
(60 Acres of Elizth Withers)				
MERCER, Geo. & James	Stafford	1773		16,197
MERCER. James, see Mercer, George				
MERCER, John Exrs.	Stafford	1768		13,236
MERCER, John Exrs.	Stafford	1773		13,236
MEREDITH, Elisha	Hanover	1763		835
MEREDITH, John*	Gloucester	1770		
MEREDITH, James	Buckingham	1773	4	
Meredith, James Jr.				
MEREDITH, James Jr., see Meredith, James				
MEREDITH, Samuel	Hanover	1763	(1762)	604
MEREDITH, Samuel	Hanover	1763		100
Do				303
MEREWETHER, Elizabeth	Hanover	1763		317
MEREWETHER, William	Hanover	1763		460
METCALF, Thomas	Gloucester	1770		
METCALF, William	Hanover	1763		37
MICKLEBERRY, Robt. Insolvent	James City	1768		
MILLAM, Edmond	Buckingham	1774	1	
MILLER, David, see Eldridge, Rolfe				
MILLER, Duncan (Kingston Par.)	Gloucester	1774	1	
MILLER, Duncan (Kingston Par.)	Gloucester	1775	1	
MILLER, Frederick	Buckingham	1774	1	
MILLER. Gabriel (Kingston Par.)	Gloucester	1774	9	
MILLER, Gabriel (Kingston Par.)	Gloucester	1775	9	
MILLER, Joseph (Kingston Par.)	Gloucester	1774	1	
MILLER, Joseph (Kingston Par.)	Gloucester	1775	1	
MILLER, Robert	James City	1768		
MILLION, Robert	Stafford	1773		229
MILLION, Robert Junr.	Stafford	1768		100
MILLION, Robert Senr.	Stafford	1768		129
MILLOM, William	Buckingham	1773	2	
Millom, Edmon				
MILLS, see Gist, Samuel				
MILLS, Charles	Hanover	1763		943
MILLS, Nicholas	Hanover	1763		280
MILLS, Robert	Gloucester	1770	1	
MILLS, Robert	Gloucester	1771	1	
MILLS, Robert	Hanover	1763		400
MILLS, Wm., see West, Edward				
MILTON, Absolom	Buckingham	1773	1	
MIMS, Drury	Buckingham	1773	8	
MIMS, Drury	Buckingham	1774	6	
MINITREE, David	James City	1768	1	
MINITREE, David	James City	1769	1	
MINOR, Thomas	Gloucester	1770	1	360
MINOR, Thomas	Gloucester	1771	6	360
MINOR, Thomas Junr.	Gloucester	1771	3	

Name	County	Year	Tithables	Acres
MINTER, James (Kingston Parish)	Gloucester	1774	1	
MINTER, James (Kingston Parish)	Gloucester	1775	1	
MINTER, Judith (Kingston Parish)	Gloucester	1774	1	
MINTER, Judith (Kingston Parish)	Gloucester	1775	1	
MISSEX, John	Hanover	1763		50
MITCHEL, James	Hanover	1763		500
MITCHELL, Isaac (Ware)*	Gloucester	1770		
MITCHELL, John*	Gloucester	1770		
MITCHEL, Joseph	Gloucester	1770	1	
MITCHEL, Richard	Gloucester	1770	1	
MITCHEL, Richard	Gloucester	1771	1	
MITCHEL, Thomas	Gloucester	1771	1	
MONCURE, John	Stafford	1768		1100
Do	In Fairfax			547
Do	In Fairfax			500
MONCURE, John	Stafford	1773		1100
Do	In Fairfax			547
Do	In Fairfax			500
MONK OF WAUGH (sic)	Stafford	1768		641
MOODY, Matthew	James City	1768	5	
MOODY, Matthew	James City	1769	2	
MOOR, William	Gloucester	1771	1	
MOORE, Alexr., see Moore, Robert				
MOORE, Augustine	James City	1768		
MOORE, Filmour	James City	1768	3	135
MOORE, Filmour	James City	1769		135
MOORE, John	Gloucester	1770		
MOORE, John	Gloucester	1771		
MOORE, Joseph	Hanover	1763	(1759)	114
MOORE, Joseph	Gloucester	1770	4	185
MOORE, Martha	James City	1768	7	26(0)
MOORE, Obededum	James City	1768	1	
MOORE, Robert Moore, Alexr.	Buckingham	1774	2	
MORCE, Martha	James City	1769	7	261
MORGAN, Edward, see Gannaway, John Jr.				
MORGAN, Haines	Gloucester	1770		
MORGAN, Richard (Kingston Par.)	Gloucester	1774		
MORGAN, Richard (Kingston Par.)	Gloucester	1775		
MORRIS, Benjamin	Hanover	1763		212
MORRIS, Benja., see Chamberlane, Richd., Capt.				
MORRIS, George	Gloucester	1770	2	
MORRIS, George	Gloucester	1771	2	
MORRIS, George	Hanover	1763		116
MORRIS, James*	Gloucester	1770		
MORRIS, James, see Gregory, Richard				
MORRIS, John	James City	1768	4	396
MORRIS, John	James City	1769	4	396
MORRIS, John (Kingston Par.)	Gloucester	1774	2	
MORRIS, John (Kingston Par.)	Gloucester	1775	2	
MORRIS, John, see Morris, Nicholas				
MORRIS, Joseph	Hanover	1763		250
MORRIS, Joshua	James City	1768	4	296
MORRIS, Joshua	James City	1769	4	296
MORRIS, Joshua	Hanover	1763	(1759)	44
MORRIS, Nicholas Morris, William	Buckingham	1773	5	
MORRIS, Nicholas Morris, John	Buckingham	1774	4	
MORRIS, Samuel	Hanover	1763		414

Name	County	Year	Tithables	Acres
MORRIS, Wm.	Buckingham	1773	1	
MORRIS, William	Gloucester	1770	4	75
MORRIS, William	Gloucester	1771	4	75
MORRIS, William	Hanover	1763		409
MORRIS, William	Hanover	1763		2650
MORRIS, William (Estate)	Gloucester	1770		25
MORRIS, William, Junr.	Buckingham	1774	1	
MORRIS, Wm., Senr.	Buckingham	1774	1	
MORRIS, William, see Morris, Nicholas				
MORROW, John	Buckingham	1773	5	
Giddeon, Francis				
Morrow, Jno. Jr.				
MORROW, John, Senr.	Buckingham	1774	5	
Morrow, Jno. Junr.				
Gideon, Francis				
MORTON, Joseph Est.	James City	1768	17	3450
MORTON, Joseph	James City	1769	17	3450
MORTON, Margret Est.	James City	1768	10	
MOSELEY, Charles	Buckingham	1773	4	
MOSELEY, Charles	Buckingham	1774	4	
MOSLEY, Francis	Buckingham	1773	9	
Evans, Joseph				
MOSELY, Francis	Buckingham	1774	12	
Payne, Benjamin				
MOSELEY, John	Buckingham	1773	7	
Godsay, Henry				
MOSLEY, John	Buckingham	1774	6	
MOSELEY, William Decd., see Cox, John Est. of				
MOSS. Edmund, see Peters, Edmund				
MOSS, James Senr.	Buckingham	1773	4	
Moss, Ray				
MOSS, James, Senr.	Buckingham	1774	4	
Moss, Ray				
MOSS, James, Junr.	Buckingham	1773	3	
MOSS, James, Junr.	Buckingham	1774	5	
Moss, Thos. Junr.				
MOSS, John (St. Martin's)	Hanover	1770	8	210
MOSS, John, see Moss, Thos., Senr.				
MOSS, John, see Johns, John				
MOSS, Ray, see Moss, James Senr.				
MOSS, Roy, (or Ray), see Moss, James Senr.				
MOSS, Thomas	Buckingham	1773	5	
Moss, John				
Moss, Thomas				
Falwell, Henry				
MOSS, Thomas	Stafford	1768		67
MOSS, Thomas	Stafford	1773		67
MOSS, Thos., Senr.	Buckingham	1774	3	
Moss, John				
MOSS, Thos. Junr., see Moss, James Junr.				
MOSS, William	Stafford	1768		133
MOSS, William	Stafford	1773		133
MOSS, William	Buckingham	1773	2	
MOSS, William	Buckingham	1774	2	
MOUNTJOY, Thomas	Stafford	1768		100
MOUNTJOY, Thomas	Stafford	1773		100
MOUNTJOY, William	Stafford	1768		1150
MOUNTJOY, William	Stafford	1773		1150
MOURNING, John	Gloucester	1770	2	
MOURNING, John	Gloucester	1771	2	

Name	County	Year	Tithables	Acres
MOYER, Peter	James City	1768	3	
MOYER, Peter	James City	1769	2	
MUCKELROY, John	Buckingham	1774	1	
MUDIE, James*	Gloucester	1770		
MULLENS, Dorothy (Kingston Par.)	Gloucester	1774		
MULLENS, Dorothy (Kingston Par.)	Gloucester	1775		
MULLINS, James (Kingston Par.)	Gloucester	1774	3	
MULLINS, James (Kingston Par.)	Gloucester	1775	3	
MUNRO, Margaret	Stafford	1773		384
"of Jno. Washington's Exrs. Better enter in Westmoreland"				
MURDOCH, Joseph	Stafford	1768		550
Do	P. William			527
MURDOCH, Joseph Exrs.	Stafford	1773		550
Do	P. William			527
MURPHEY, John, see Murphey, Thomas Truman				
MURPHY, Peter	Stafford	1768		258
MURPHY, Peter	Stafford	1773		258
MURPHEY, Richd., see Murphey, Thomas Truman				
MURPHEY, Thomas Truman	Buckingham	1773	3	
Murphey, John				
Murphey, Truman				
MURPHEY, Thomas Truman	Buckingham	1774	4	
Murphey, Truman				
Murphey, John				
Murphey, Richd.				
MURRAY, James Foun(tain)	Gloucester	1770	9	700
MURREL, James, see Pryer, David				
MURREL, Thomas	Buckingham	1773	2	
MURREL, Wilkerson, see Thomas, Joseph				
MURRY, Anthony	Buckingham	1773	14	
Saunderson, John				
MURRY, Anthony	Buckingham	1774	14	
Hencan, John				
MURRY, Laurance	Buckingham	1774	1	
MURRY, Laurance, see Hardwick, George				
MUTTLOW, James, Esta.	James City	1768		150
MUTTLOW, William	James City	1768	1	80
MUTTLOW, William	James City	1769	2	80
NAPIER, Elizabeth	Hanover	1763		100
NAUGHTON, George	Gloucester	1770	4	133
NAUGHTON, George	Gloucester	1771	2	133
NAUGHTON, Geo., see Wiatt, Peter				
NEEL, Wm., see Lee, Evan				
NEIGHBORS, Francis	Buckingham	1774	1	
NAILE, Wm., see Watkins, Joel				
NELSON, Edward	Hanover	1763		350
Do				315
NELSON, James	Hanover	1763		735
NELSON, John, see Cary, Archibald Col.				
NELSON, Thomas	Hanover	1763		680
NELSON, Thomas	Gloucester	1770		
NELSON, William, Esqr.	Hanover	1763		14,850
NELSON, Wm., Esqr.	James City	1768		225
NEW, John	Gloucester	1770	4	87
NEW, John	Gloucester	1771	4	87
NEW, Daniel	Gloucester	1770	7	127
		His mother's		181
NEW, Daniel	Gloucester	1771	10	127

Name	County	Year	Tithables	Acres
NEW, Daniel	Gloucester	1771	10	308
NEW, Daniel, Junr.	Gloucester	1771		
NEW, James	Gloucester	1770	1	110
NEW, James	Gloucester	1771		110
NEWCOMB, John	Gloucester	1771	3	
NEWELL, George	James City	1768	5	150
NEWELL, George	James City	1769	6	150
NEWMAN, John	James City	1768	1	
NEWMAN, John	James City	1769	1	
NETHERLAND, Charles	Hanover	1763		234
NETTLES, Robert	Gloucester	1770	1	75
NETTLES, Robert	Gloucester	1771	2	75
NICHOLAS, Elisha	Gloucester	1771	1	
NICHOLAS, John	Buckingham	1773	38	
Johnston, John				
Jefferson, Randolph				
Campbell, Patrick				
McCallum, Daniel				
Taylor, Samuel Jur.				
Perkins, Walker				
Bootwright, Jesse				
NICHOLAS, John	Buckingham	1774	34	
Campbell, Peter				
McCallum, Danl.				
NICHOLAS, Robert Carter Esqr.	James City	1768	12	450
"also 10 tithes at your quarter"				
NICHOLAS, Robert C.	James City	1769	19	450
"to 11 tithes Jas. City Parish"				
NICHOLSON, Edwd. Estate	James City	1768		200
NICHOLSON, George	Stafford	1768		50
NICHOLSON, George	Stafford	1773		50
NIMMO, David	Hanover	1763		250
Do N(ew) Pat.(ent) for 248 first due for 1764"				
NORMAN, Thomas	Stafford	1768		300
NORMAN, Thomas	Stafford	1773		300
NORRIS, John	Stafford	1768		275
NORRIS, John	Stafford	1773		275
NORTH, Richard	Buckingham	1773	2	
NORTH, Richard	Buckingham	1774	2	
NORTHCUTT, Richard	Buckingham	1773	1	
NORTHCUT, Richard	Buckingham	1774	1	
NORTHCUT, William	Buckingham	1774	2	
Northcutt, Terry				
NORVELL, William	James City	1768	15	851
NORVELL, William	James City	1769	14	851
NORWELL, George	Hanover	1763		282
NORWELL, James	Hanover	1763	(1756)	300
NOWLIN, James	Buckingham	1773	3	
Elsom, Thomas				
NOWLING, Francis	Buckingham	1774	2	
Nowling, Richd.				
NUCKOLS, James	Hanover	1763		126
NUCKOLS, Samuel	Hanover	1763		200
NUCUM, John	Buckingham	1773	1	
NUTTALL, George	Gloucester	1770	8	163
NUTTALL, George	Gloucester	1771	6	163
NUTTALL, Hazlum	Gloucester	1770		
NUTTALL, Hazlum	Gloucester	1771		
NUTTALL, James	Gloucester	1770	2	180
NUTTALL, James	Gloucester	1771	2	180

Name	County	Year	Tith-ables	Acres
NUTTALL, John	Gloucester	1770	6	
NUTTALL, John	Gloucester	1771	5	
NUTTALL, Mary	Gloucester	1770	3	
NUTTALL, Mary	Gloucester	1771	4	
NUTTALL, Matthias	Gloucester	1770		
NUTTALL, Matthias	Gloucester	1771	3	
NUTTALL, Thomas	Gloucester	1770	2	
NUTTALL, Thomas	Gloucester	1771	4	
OAKLEY, Benjamin	Hanover	1763		33
OBRIAN, Matthias	Buckingham	1773	1	
OBRIAN, Patrick	Buckingham	1773	1	
OGLESBY, David, see Perkins, Hardin				
OGLESBY, Shadrick, see Cox, John Hartwell				
OGLESBY, Shadrack, see Cocke, Hartwell Col., Est.				
OLIVER, Benjamin	Hanover	1763		594
OLIVER, James*	Gloucester	1770		
ORR, _____, see Greenless, _____				
OVERSTREET, James	Hanover	1763		72
OVERTON, Samuel	Hanover	1763		1095
OVERTON, William	Hanover	1763		1095
OVERWHARTON PARISH of P. Daniel	Stafford	1768		100
OWEN, Ann (Kingston Par.)	Gloucester	1774		
OWEN, Ann (Kingston Par.)	Gloucester	1775		
OWEN, George (Kingston Par.)	Gloucester	1774	1	
OWEN, George (Kingston Par.)	Gloucester	1775	1	
OWEN, William (Kingston Par.)	Gloucester	1774		
OWEN, William (Kingston Par.)	Gloucester	1775		
OZENBRIGGS, Richd.	Gloucester	1770	2	
OZENBRIGGS, Richd.	Gloucester	1771	1	
PAGE, John	Buckingham	1773	1	
PAGE, John	Buckingham	1774	1	
PAGE, John, the Hona^{bl}	Gloucester	1771		1679
PAGE. John Jr.	Gloucester	1770	78	2000
PAGE, John Jr.	Gloucester	1771	80	2000
PAGE, John Senr.	Gloucester	1770	67	2679
PAGE, John Senr.	Gloucester	1771	75	2679
PAGE, Mann	Stafford	1773		4016
PAGE, Mann (Kingston Par.)	Gloucester	1774	14	
PAGE, Mann (Kingston Par.)	Gloucester	1775	14	
PAGE, Mann, Esqr.	Hanover	1763		950
PAGE, Mann, Junr.	Gloucester	1770		950
PAGE, Mann Senr.	Gloucester	1770	43 45	3515
PAGE, Robert	Hanover	1763		2258
PAGE, Robert, see King, _____				
PAISLEY, John	Hanover	1763		200
PALISTER, John (Kingston Par.)	Gloucester	1774	2	
PALISTER, John (Kingston Par.)	Gloucester	1775	2	
PALMER, George Palmer, Wm.	Buckingham	1773	2	
PALMER, James	Buckingham	1773	1	
PALMER, James	Buckingham	1774	1	
PALMER, Nixon	Buckingham	1773	1	
PALMER, Wm.	Buckingham	1774	2	
PALMER, William	Gloucester	1770	1	

Name	County	Year	Tithables	Acres
PALMER, William	Gloucester	1771	1	
PALMER, Wm., see Palmer, George				
PALMOR, Isaac, see Palmor, John Senr.				
PALMOR, James	Buckingham	1773	2	
PALMOR, John	Buckingham	1773	4	
Palmor, Isaac				
PALMOR, John	Buckingham	1774	5	
Palmor, Isaac				
PALMOR, John, Junr.	Buckingham	1773	1	
PALMORE, John	Buckingham	1774	3	
PAMER, Nixon, see Saunders, Daniel				
PAMPLIN, James (Tillotson Par.)	Buckingham	1773	5	
PARRIS, Samuel (St. Martin's)	Hanover	1770	1	200
PARROTT, John (Kingston Par.)	Gloucester	1774	2	
PARROTT, John (Kingston Par.)	Gloucester	1775	2	
PARROTT, Martha	James City	1769	1	177
PARSONS, James (Kingston Par.)	Gloucester	1774	2	
PARSONS, James (Kingston Par.)	Gloucester	1775	2	
PARSONS, John (Kingston Par.)	Gloucester	1774	6	
PARSONS, John (Kingston Par.)	Gloucester	1775	6	
PASLEY, Richard	Buckingham	1773	1	
PASLEY, Richard, see Garratt, Charles, dec'd Estate				
PASTURE, William	James City	1768	9	
PASTURE, William	James City	1769	7	
PATE, Jacob, see Pate, Obediah				
PATE, Matthew	Hanover	1763		200
PATE, Obediah (Bro. of Jacob)	Gloucester	1770	1	
PATE, Obediah (Bro. of Jacob)	Gloucester	1771	1	
PATE, Thomas	James City	1768	3	
PATE, Thomas	James City	1(?)		
PATE, Thomas	James City	1769	3	413
PATERSON, James	Hanover	1763		100
PATRICK, Daniel	Hanover	1763		159
PATTESON, Ben, see Patteson, Peter				
PATTESON, Charles	Buckingham	1773	6	
Patterson, Le__(a)(mutilated)				
PATTESON, Charles (Tillotson Par.)	Buckingham	1773	4	
PATTESON, Charles (Tillotson Par.)	Buckingham	1774	4	
PATTESON, Charles	Buckingham	1774	6	
Patteson, Landis				
PATTESON, David (Tillotson Par.)	Buckingham	1773	9	
Edins, John				
PATTESON, David (Tillotson Par.)	Buckingham	1774	10	
Edins, John				
PATTESON, David, see Patteson, John				
PATTESON, David Estate	Buckingham	1774	6	
Patteson, Jno.				
PATTESON, James	Buckingham	1773	2	
PATTESON, James	Buckingham	1774	4	
PATTESON, John	Buckingham	1773	8	
PATTESON, John "Clerk"	Buckingham	1774	1	
PATTESON, John	Buckingham	1774	8	
PATTESON, Jno., see Patteson, David Estate				
PATTESON, John	Buckingham	1773	5	
Belonging to Estate of David Patteson				
PATTESON, Landis, see Patteson, Charles				
PATTERSON, Le__(a) (mutilated), see Patterson, Charles				
PATTESON, Littleberry	Buckingham	1774	1	
PATTESON, Peter	Buckingham	1773	4	
Patteson, Ben				

Name	County	Year	Tithables	Acres
PATTESON, Peter	Buckingham	1774	3	
PATTESON, Thomas	Buckingham	1773	5	
Gilliam, Archr.				
PATTESON, Thos.	Buckingham	1774	6	
Lee, Wm.				
PATTESON, Thomas	Buckingham	1773	7	
Shepherd, Wm.				
PATTESON, Thomas	Buckingham	1774	7	
Shepherd, Wm.				
PATTESON, Wm., Junr.	Buckingham	1774	1	
PAYNE, Barnett	Buckingham	1773	1	
PAYNE, Barnett	Buckingham	1774	1	
PAYNE, Benjamin, see Moseley, Francis				
PAYNE, Benja., see Stinson, John				
PAYNE, Daniel (of Thos. Ashby)	Stafford	1768		78
PAYNE, Daniel	Stafford	1773		78
PAYNE, Joseph	Buckingham	1773	1	
PAYNE, Joseph	Buckingham	1774	1	
PAYNE, William	Hanover	1763		200
PEACE, Lucy	Hanover	1763		100
PEACE, Joseph	Hanover	1763		95
PEACE, Sarah	Hanover	1763		33
PEAD, John, see Thornbury, Samuel				
PEAK, Henry	Buckingham	1773	3	
PEAK, Henry	Buckingham	1774	3	
PEAK, Jeffery	Buckingham	1773	1	
PEAK, Jeffery	Buckingham	1774	2	
PEAKE, Migale	Hanover	1763		60
PEAKE, William	Buckingham	1773	1	
PEARCE, John	Hanover	1763		804
PEARMAN, Mary	James City	1768		
PEASLEY, Wm.	Buckingham	1774	3	
PEASLEY, Revert. William	Buckingham	1773	3	
PEATERS, Jasper insolvent	James City	1768	2	
PEED, James (Kingston Par.)	Gloucester	1774	4	
PEED, James (Kingston Par.)	Gloucester	1775	4	
PEED, James, Junr.	Gloucester	1774	1	
Kingston Parish				
PEED, James, Junr.	Gloucester	1775	1	
Kingston Parish				
PEED, Lewis, Senr.	Gloucester	1774	2	
Kingston Parish				
PEED, Lewis, Senr.	Gloucester	1775	2	
Kingston Parish				
PEED, Lewis, Junr.	Gloucester	1774	1	
Kingston Parish				
PEED, Lewis, Junr.	Gloucester	1775	1	
Kingston Parish				
PEED, William (Kingston Par.)	Gloucester	1774	1	
PEED, William (Kingston Par.)	Gloucester	1775	1	
PEEK, John	Buckingham	1774	3	
Peek, Aaron				
Peek, Jonathan				
PEEK, John Junr.	Buckingham	1773	3	
Peek, Aaron				
Peek, Absolom				
PEEK, Jonathan, see Peek, John				
PEEK, Wm.	Buckingham	1774	1	
PEEK, Thomas (Kingston Par.)	Gloucester	1774	1	
PEEK, Thomas (Kingston Par.)	Gloucester	1775	1	

Name	County	Year	Tithables	Acres
PEGRUM, Elizabeth	James City	1769	2	
PEGRUM, John	James City	1768	3	
PELHAM, Peter	James City	1768	5	
PELHAM, Peter	James City	1769	6	
PEN, Rawly (Mulatto)	Buckingham	1774	1	
½ENDLETON, Benja.	Buckingham	1774	1	
PENDLETON, Ben, see Freeland, Mace				
PENDLETON, John	Buckingham	1773	1	
PENDLETON, John, see Freeland, Mace				
PENIX, Joseph	Hanover	1763		120
PENNINGTON, Anne	James City	1768	4	
PENNINGTON, Anne	James City	1769	4	
PEPER, Nathan	James City	1768	2	100
PEPPIN, Richd.*	Gloucester	1770		
PEPPIN, Banister	Gloucester	1770		
PERRY, John	James City	1769	1	
PERKINS, Baker	James City	1769	6	100
PERKINS, George	Gloucester	1770		
PERKINS, Hardin	Buckingham	1773	9	
Oglesby, David				
PERKINS, Hardin	Buckingham	1774	10	
PERKINS, Henry, see Wright, George				
PERKINS, John	Hanover	1763		60
PERKINS, John W., see Perkins, William Senr.				
PERKINS, John Watkins, see Perkins, William				
PERKINS, Walker, see Nicholas, John				
PERKINS, William	Buckingham	1773	4	
Perkins, John Watkins				
PERKINS, William Junr.	Buckingham	1773	4	
PERKINS, Wm.	Buckingham	1774	5	
PERKINS, William Senr.	Buckingham	1774	4	
Perkins, John W.				
PERRIN, Henry	Hanover	1763		50
Do				50
PERRIN, John	Gloucester	1770	46	2244
Do				200
PERRIN, John	Gloucester	1771	54	2244
Do				200
PERRIN, Mary	Gloucester	1770	5	
PERRIN, Mary	Gloucester	1771	5	
PERRIN, Thomas (Estate)*	Gloucester	1770		
PERROW, Charles	Buckingham	1773	7	
Perrow, Daniel				
Perrow, Charles, Junr.				
PERROW, Charles	Buckingham	1774	7	
Perrow, Daniel				
Perrow, Charles, Junr.				
PERROW, Daniel	Buckingham	1773	6	
Perrow, Daniel Battersby				
Perrow, Stephen				
PERROW, Daniel	Buckingham	1774	6	
Perrow, Stephen				
Perrow, Danl. B.				
PERROW, Daniel, see Perrow, Charles				
PETERS, Edmund	Buckingham	1774	5	
Moss, Edmund				
PETERS, James (of Wood)	Stafford	1768		465
PETERS, James (of Wood)	Stafford	1773		465
(100 Acres sold to Marias Hansbrough"				
PETTUS, George	Hanover	1763		650

Name	County	Year	Tithables	Acres
PETTUS, John (St. Martin's)	Hanover	1770	9	960
PETTUS, Stephen	Hanover	1763		500
PETTUS, William (St. Martin's)	Hanover	1770	6	
PEYTON, John (Kingston Par.)	Gloucester	1774	49	
PEYTON, John (Kingston Par.)	Gloucester	1775	49	
PEYTON, John Exrs.	Stafford	1773		5159

"will not make any payment, as they say they are uncertain whether they have any land until the present dispute with G. Britain is settled."

Name	County	Year	Tithables	Acres
PEYTON, John, Exrs.	Stafford	1768		5159
PHELPS, John Anglin, Adrian	Buckingham	1773	4	
PHELPS, John Burton, Jacob Stanton, Matthew	Buckingham	1774	5	
PHELPS, Richd., see Phelps, Wm.				
PHELPS, Thomas	Buckingham	1774	3	
PHELPS, Thomas Phelps, Josiah	Buckingham	1773	4	
PHELPS, Wm. Phelps, Richd.	Buckingham	1773	4	
PHELPS, Wm. Phelps, Richd.	Buckingham	1774	4	
PHILIPS, John	Hanover	1763		450
PHILIPS, Nathan	Hanover	1763		250
Do				100
PHILLUPS, Elizabeth	Gloucester	1770	1	
PHILLUPS, Elizabeth	Gloucester	1771	1	
PHILLPOTTS, Benjamin	Gloucester	1770	2	
PHILLPOTS, Oakley	Gloucester	1770	2	
PHILLPOTS, Oakley	Gloucester	1771	2	
PIGG, William	Hanover	1763		211
PIGG, William	James City	1768		
PIGGET, John	James City	1768	1	
PIGGET, John	James City	1769	1	
PIGOTT, Pearson	James City	1768	3	191 or 171
PIGGOTT, Pearson	James City	1769	4	369
PILCHER, Stephen	Stafford	1768		100
PILCHER, Stephen	Stafford	1773		100
PITT, George	Hanover	1763		650
PITT, George	James City	1768	8	100
PITT, George	James City	1769	5	100
PITTS, Benjamin	Gloucester	1771	1	
PITTS, Peter	Gloucester	1770	5	
PITTS, Peter	Gloucester	1771	4	
PLANT, Williamson	Hanover	1763		200
PLUMMER, George Wm.(Kingston Par.)	Gloucester	1774	4	
PLUMMER, George Wm.(Kingston Par.)	Gloucester	1775	4	
PLUMMER, Judith (Kingston Par.)	Gloucester	1774	6	
PLUMMER, Judith (Kingston Par.)	Gloucester	1775	6	
PLUMMER, William (Kingston Par.)	Gloucester	1774	16	
PLUMMER, William (Kingston Par.)	Gloucester	1775	16	
PLUMMER, William Junr. Kingston Parish	Gloucester	1774	1	
PLUMMER, William Junr. Kingston Parish	Gloucester	1775	1	
POINTER, Elizabeth*	Gloucester	1770		
POINTER, Henry	Gloucester	1770	8	384
POINTER, Henry	Gloucester	1771	6	384

Name	County	Year	Tithables	Acres
POINTER, James	Gloucester	1771	1	
POINTER, Michael	Gloucester	1770	3	
POINTER, Michael	Gloucester	1771	4	
POLLARD, William	Hanover	1763		890
POLLARD, William	Gloucester	1770	7	82
POLLARD, William	Gloucester	1771	8	82
POMPROY, Robert	Gloucester	1771	2	
POOLE, Thomas (Kingston Par.)	Gloucester	1774	5	
POOLE, Thomas (Kingston Par.)	Gloucester	1775	5	
POOR, Adam	Hanover	1763		144
POPE, ____, see Gerrard, Wm.				
POPE, Hum., see Gerrard, Wm.				
PORCH, Thomas	Stafford	1768		80
PORCH, Thomas	Stafford	1773		80
PORCH, William	Stafford	1768		80
PORREAR, Hezekiah	Hanover	1763		200
PORTER, ____, Exrs., see Ralls, John				
PORTER, Calvert	Stafford	1768		145
PORTER, Calvert	Stafford	1773		145
PORTER, Nichs. (of Benj. Brent)	Stafford	1768		400
PORTER, Nick., Exrs.	Stafford	1773		400
PORTER, Thomas, Exrs.	Stafford	1768		200
PORTER, Thomas, Exrs.	Stafford	1773		200
POWELL, Benjamin	James City	1768	8 & 6	460
POWELL, Benjamin "to 11 tithes"	James City	1769	6	1012
POWELL, Edmond Senr.	Gloucester	1771	1	
POWELL, Edmd. Junr.	Gloucester	1771	1	
POWELL, George	Gloucester	1770	5	
POWELL, George	Gloucester	1771	4	
POWELL, Henry (Kingston Par.)	Gloucester	1774	2	
POWELL, Henry (Kingston Par.)	Gloucester	1775		
POWELL, Hudson	Gloucester	1768	1	
Do		1769	1	
Do		1770	3	
Do		1771	3	
POWELL, James	Gloucester	1770	1	
POWELL, James	Gloucester	1771	1	
POWELL, John (Kingston Par.)	Gloucester	1774	1	
POWELL, John (Kingston Par.)	Gloucester	1775	1	
POWELL, Lucas	James City	1768		
POWELL, Thomas*	Gloucester	1770		
POWER, Allice	James City	1769	7	
POWER, Edward	James City	1768	19	881
POWER, Edward	James City	1769	10	881
POWER, John	Hanover	1763		1000
POWER, John	James City	1768	13	800
POWER, John	James City	1769	12	800
POWERS, Major	Hanover	1763		210
PRATT, ____, see Etherington, Daniel				
PRATT, Thomas (Exrs. of Helen's) "Say they never purchased this land"	Stafford	1773		100
PRATT, Thomas Exrs.	Stafford	1768		2261
PRATT, Thomas Exrs. "200 Acres sold to Daniel Etherington"	Stafford	1773		2161
PRENTIS, John Col.	James City	1768		
PRENTIS, Mary	James City	1768	12	430
PRENTIS, Mary	James City	1769	13	430
THE PRESBETERIAN (sic) CONGREGATION	Hanover	1763		210
PRETCHARD, John	Buckingham	1773	1	

Name	County	Year	Tithables	Acres
PREWIT, James	James City	1769	1	
PREWIT, Peter	James City	1768		
PREWIT, William	James City	1768		150
PREWIT, William	James City	1769	3	150
PRICE, Thomas	James City	1768		
PRICE, Thomas	Stafford	1768		200
PRICE, Thomas	Stafford	1773		200
Do		of Wheeler		100
(The 100 acres lies in Westmoreland Co.)				
PRICE, Thos., see Wheeler, William				
PRIDE, Francis	Buckingham	1774	4	
PRIDE, James Esqr.	James City	1768	22	1600
PRIDE, James Esqr.	James City	1769	18	1600
PRINCE, Silvanus	James City	1768	7	575
PRINCE, Silvanus	James City	1769	8	575
PRICE, John	Hanover	1763		1375
Do				193
PRICE, John	Gloucester	1770	4	
PRICE, Ghomas	Gloucester	1770	12	550
PRICE, Thomas	Gloucester	1771	14	550
PRICHARD, John	Buckingham	1774	1	
PRIDDY, George	Hanover	1763		300
PRIDDY, Robert	Hanover	1763		450
PRIOR, Robert	Hanover	1763		350
PRIOR, Ann	Gloucester	1770	1	
PRIOR, Samuel	Hanover	1763		485
PROCTER, Richard	Gloucester	1770	1	
PROCTER, Richard	Gloucester	1771	1	
PROSSER, Elizabeth	Hanover	1763		439
PRYER, David	Buckingham	1773	3	
Murrel, James				
PRYER, David	Buckingham	1774	1	
PRYER, Edmd. (Edwd.)	Buckingham	1774	2	
PRYER, Edward	Buckingham	1773	3	
Smith, N__cy (mutilated)				
PRYER, John, see Bernard, John				
PRYER, Sarah	Buckingham	1773	3	
Jenning, William				
PEYER, Sarah	Buckingham	1774	2	
PEYER, William	Buckingham	1773	1	
PRYER, William	Buckingham	1774	1	
PUCKET, Robert	Buckingham	1773	1	
PUGH, Elias (Kingston Par.)	Gloucester	1774	1	
PUGH, Elias (Kingston Par.)	Gloucester	1775	1	
PUGH, William (Kingston Par.)	Gloucester	1774	2	
PUGH, William (Kingston Par.)	Gloucester	1775	2	
PULLER, James, Senr.	Gloucester	1770		
PULLER, James, Jr.*	Gloucester	1770		
PULLER, Joseph*	Gloucester	1770		
PULLER, Ledford	Gloucester	1771	1	
PULLIAM, Drury	Hanover	1763		200
PULLIAM, Zachariah	Hanover	1763		75
PURDIE & DIXON Messieurs	Gloucester	1770		
PURDIE, George	James City	1768		
PURNAL, John (Kingston Par.)	Gloucester	1774	1	
PURNAL, John (Kingston Par.)	Gloucester	1775	1	
PURSELL, Harry	Gloucester	1770	10	185
PURSELL, Harry	Gloucester	1771	8	185
PURSELL, William	Gloucester	1770	8	394
PURSELL, William	Gloucester	1771	8	394

Name	County	Year	Tithables	Acres
QUALLS, David	Buckingham	1774	1	
QUALLS, John	Buckingham	1773	1	
QUALLS, John	Buckingham	1774	1	
RADFORD, John	Buckingham	1774	1	
RADFORD, John, see Webb, Theodorick				
RAGLAND, Anne	Hanover	1763		250
RAGLAND, John (St. Martin's)	Hanover	1770	6	600
RAGLAND, John, decd. (St. Martin's)	Hanover	1770	0	1090
RAGLAND, Pettus	Hanover	1763		383
RAGLAND, Rueben	Hanover	1763		166
RAGLAND, Saml. (St. Martin's)	Hanover	1770	12	1510
RAILEY, Philip	Buckingham	1774	1	
RAILEY, Shelton, see Goss, James				
RAKES, Charles	Buckingham	1774	1	
RAKES, Charles, see Garrott, Stephen				
RAKES, David	Buckingham	1773	1	
RAKES, Henry	Buckingham	1774	1	
Rakes, David				
RAKES, William	Buckingham	1773	1	
RAKES, William	Buckingham	1774	1	
RALEY, Shelton, see Goss, James				
RALLS, John	Stafford	1768		2397
Do	of Porter's Exrs.			100
Do	of John Saunders			250
RALLS, John	Stafford	1773		2397
	of Porter's Exrs.			100
	of John Saunders			250
RALLS, John Junr.	Stafford	1768		747
RALLS, John Junr.	Stafford	1773		747
RAMSEY, Benjamin	James City	1768	3	
"300 Acres for G. Keeling"				
RAMSEY, Morris	James City	1768	5	215
RAMSEY, Morris	James City	1769	6	215
RAMSEY, William	Gloucester	1771	1	
RANDOLPH, Agatha	Gloucester	1770	18	767
RANDOLPH, Agatha	Gloucester	1771	22	767
RANDOLPH, John Esqr.	James City	1768	12	100
RANDOLPH, John	James City	1769	7	100
"to 13 Tithes"				
RANDOLPH, Peyton Esqr.	James City	1768	17 & 6	1671
RANDOLPH, Peyton	James City	1769	7	1671
"to 16 tithes"				
RANSON, Richard	Gloucester	1770	9	160
RANSON, Richard	Gloucester	1771	9	160
RANSONE, Augustin	Gloucester	1770	3	
RANSONE, Augustin	Gloucester	1771	5	
(Pe. by his father)				
RANSONE, Flamsteed	Buckingham	1774	6	
Ransone, Henry				
RANSONE, Peter	Gloucester	1770	3	
RANSONE, Peter	Gloucester	1771	3	
RATCHFORD, William	Gloucester	1770	2	
RATCHFORD, William	Gloucester	1771	4	
RATLIFF, John	James City	1769		
RAWLEY, James (St. Martin's)	Hanover	1770	1	
RAWLEY, John	James City	1768	4	100
RAWLEY, John	James City	1769	4	100
RAWLY, James	Hanover	1763		65

Name	County	Year	Tithables	Acres
RAYLEY, Thomas	Hanover	1763	(1762)	150
RAYLEY, Wm.	Buckingham	1773	1	
READ, Philip	Hanover	1763		90
REAVES, Jane (Kingston Par.)	Gloucester	1774		
REAVES, Jane (Kingston Par.)	Gloucester	1775		
REDD, Thomas	Buckingham	1773	6	
REDD, Thomas	Buckingham	1774	10	
Redd, John				
REDWOOD, John	James City	1769	1	
REED, Robert	James City	1768		
RENNO, John, see Rennoe, Stephen				
RENNE, Stephen	Buckingham	1774	1	
RENOLDS, Archer	Buckingham	1773	2	
Renolds, Moses				
RENNOE, Stephen	Buckingham	1773	2	
Renno, John				
RESPESS, Richard (Kingston Par.)	Gloucester	1774	4	
RESPESS, Richard (Kingston Par.)	Gloucester	1775	4	
RESPESS, Thomas, Junr. Kingston Parish	Gloucester	1774	5	
RESPESS, Thomas, Junr. Kingston Parish	Gloucester	1775	5	
RESPESS, William (Kingston Par.)	Gloucester	1774	4	
RESPESS, William (Kingston Par.)	Gloucester	1775	4	
REVES, John	Buckingham	1773	1	
REYNOLDS, Archelus	Buckingham	1774	2	
Reynolds, Moses				
REYNOLDS, Charles	Buckingham	1774	1	
REYNOLDS, David, overseer, see Cabell, Joseph, Col.				
REYNOLDS, Moses, see Reynolds, Archelus				
RHODES, William	James City	1768		
RICE, Clifton	Hanover	1763		200
RICE, David	Hanover	1763		200
RICE, John	Hanover	1763		212
RICE, Thomas	Hanover	1763		120
Do				250
RICHARDSON, Charles	Hanover	1763		246
RICHARDSON, David	Hanover	1763		591
Do				1072
RICHARDSON, David (St. Martin's)	Hanover	1770	6	
RICHARDSON, David, Junr. St. Martin's	Hanover	1770	4	466
RICHARDSON, Dudley	James City	1768	10	270
RICHARDSON, Dudley	James City	1769	10	270
RICHARDSON, Elizabeth	James City	1769	1	100
RICHARDSON, John	Hanover	1763		300
RICHARDSON, Richard	Hanover	1763		100
Do				300
RICHARDSON, Samuel	Stafford	1768		750
RICHARDSON, Samuel	Stafford	1773		750
RICHARDSON, Stanup	Hanover	1763		150
RICHARDSON, Stanup, see Johns, John				
RICHARDSON, Turner	Hanover	1763		300
RICHARDSON, William	James City	1768	12	596
RICHARDSON, William	James City	1769	13	596
RICHMAN, John	Hanover	1763		100
RICHIN. ESTATE, see Walker, Otey				
RIDDLE, Matthew	Hanover	1763		100
RIDER, Abraham	Gloucester	1770	1	
Paid by William Rider				

Name	County	Year	Tithables	Acres
RIDER, Abraham	Gloucester	1771	1	
Paid by William Rider				
RIDER, James	Gloucester	1770	1	
RIDER, James	Gloucester	1771	1	
RIDER, William	Gloucester	1770	1	
RIDER, William	Gloucester	1771	1	
RIDER, William, see Rider, Abraham				
RIDGEWAY, James	Buckingham	1774	2	
RIDGEWAY, Phebe	Buckingham	1773	3	
RIDGEWAY, Phebey	Buckingham	1774	3	
Fanning, Harry				
RIDGEWAY, Richard	Buckingham	1774	2	
RIDGWAY, John	Buckingham	1773		
RIDGWAY, Richd.	Buckingham	1773	2	
RIGBY, Jean	Stafford	1768		50
RIGBY, Jean	Stafford	1773		50
RIGHT, Augustin	Buckingham	1773	1	
RIGHT, John	Buckingham	1773	1	
RILIE, William	Gloucester	1770		
RIPLEY, John (Kingston Par.)	Gloucester	1774	3	
RIPLEY, John (Kingston Par.)	Gloucester	1775		
RIPPLEY, Richard	Buckingham	1773	3	
RIPPLY, Richd.	Buckingham	1774	3	
ROAN, Alexander	Gloucester	1770	2	166
ROAN, Alexander	Gloucester	1771	2	166
ROBERSON, James, see Taylor, Samuel, Junr.				
ROBERTS, Matt insolvent	James City	1768	1	
ROBERTS, William	Gloucester	1770	4	
ROBERTS, William	Gloucester	1771	6	
ROBERTS, Eliza.	James City	1769	1	
ROBERTSON, James, see Taylor, Joseph				
ROBERTSON, Mary	Buckingham	1773	1	
ROBERTSON, Mary	Buckingham	1774	1	
ROBERTSON, Richard	Buckingham	1773	1	
ROBERTSON, Zachariah	Buckingham	1774	1	
ROBINS, Albin (Kingston Par.)	Gloucester	1774	3	
ROBINS, Albin (Kingston Par.)	Gloucester	1775	3	
ROBINS, Edmund (Kingston Par.)	Gloucester	1774	1	
ROBINS, Edmund (Kingston Par.)	Gloucester	1775	1	
ROBINS, John	Gloucester	1770	3	136
ROBINS, John	Gloucester	1771	3	136
ROBINS, John, see Robins, William				
ROBINS, Peter (Kingston Par.)	Gloucester	1774	1	
ROBINS, Peter (Kingston Par.)	Gloucester	1775	1	
ROBINS, Thomas	Gloucester	1770	6	
ROBINS, Thomas	Gloucester	1771	4	
ROBINS, William (father of John)	Gloucester	1770	10	1000
ROBINS, William (father of John)	Gloucester	1771	11	1000
ROBINS, William (Kingston Par.)	Gloucester	1774	1	
ROBINS, William (Kingston Par.)	Gloucester	1775	1	
ROBINS, William, Junr.	Gloucester	1770	1	
ROBINS, William, Junr.	Gloucester	1771	2	
ROBINSON, Benjamin	Stafford	1768		700
(50 Acres of Henry Robinson Exrs.)				
ROBINSON, Benjamin	Gloucester	1770	1	
(pd. John Robinson's Co. Levy)				
ROBINSON, Benjamin	Gloucester	1771	1	
(Pd. John Robinson's Co. Levy)				
ROBINSON, Benjamin	Stafford	1773		700
Do 50 Acres from Henry Robison Exrs.				

Name	County	Year	Tith-ables	Acres
ROBINSON, Benj., see Robinson, John				
ROBINSON, Charles	Gloucester	1770	2	
ROBINSON, Cristopher (sic)	Stafford	1768		50
of Henry Robinson Exrs.				
ROBINSON, Christopher	Stafford	1773		50
ROBINSON, Christopher	James City	1768	13	700
ROBINSON, Christopher	James City	1769	12	700
ROBINSON, H(en)ry	Hanover	1763		620
ROBINSON, Henry's Exors., see Robinson, Benjamin				
ROBINSON, Joh(n) Esqr.	Hanover	1763		3866
ROBINSON, John	Gloucester	1770	5	95
ROBINSON, John	Gloucester	1771	5	95
(Pd. for Benj. Robinson)				
ROBINSON, John (Kingston Par.)	Gloucester	1774	18	
ROBINSON, John (Kingston Par.)	Gloucester	1775	18	
ROBINSON, John, see Robinson, Benjamin				
ROBINSON, Henry, see Robinson, Benjamin				
ROBY, William (of Simon Thomas	Stafford	1768		200
Do	of John Grigsby			300
Do	of William Grigsby			100
ROE, Mary	Gloucester	1770	1	
ROE, Mary	Gloucester	1771	1	
ROGERS, Giles	Hanover	1763	(1759)	843
ROGERS, James	James City	1768	2	190
ROGERS, James	James City	1769	2	190
ROGERS, John	James City	1768	3	
ROGERS, John	James City	1768		
ROGERS, John	James City	1769	2	
ROGERS, William	James City	1769	5	
ROLLISON, John	James City	1768	6	
ROLLISON, John	James City	1769	6	
ROOTS, John	Gloucester	1770	18	1020
ROOTS, John	Gloucester	1771	18	1020
ROSARRO, Mary insolvent	James City	1768	1	
ROSBERRY, wm., see Bostick, John				
ROSEBERRY, William	Buckingham	1773	1	
ROSE, William	James City	1768	1	
ROSS, Francis	Gloucester	1770	1	
ROUNTREE, William	Hanover	1763	(1759)	250
ROUT, George	Stafford	1768		250
ROUT, George	Stafford	1773		250
ROUT, Peter, Exrs.	Stafford	1768		714
ROUTON, John	Buckingham	1773	3	
Williams, Robin				
ROUTON, John	Buckingham	1774	4	
Williams, Rubin				
ROW, Banister	Gloucester	1770	2	200
ROW, Banister	Gloucester	1771	2	200
ROW, Hansford	Gloucester	1770	5	
ROW, Hansford	Gloucester	1771	5	
ROW, Joseph*	Gloucester	1770		
ROW, Rebecca	Gloucester	1770		500
ROW, Rebecca	Gloucester	1771		500
ROW, Rebecca, see Row, Zachariah				
ROW, Thomas (Estate)	Gloucester	1770	7	700
ROW, Thomas (Estate)	Gloucester	1771	8	350
ROW, William	Hanover	1763	(1756)	300
ROW, William	Gloucester	1770	23	200
ROW, William	Gloucester	1771	25	700
ROW, Zachariah	Gloucester	1770	7	

Name	County	Year	Tithables	Acres
Son of Rebecca Row				
ROW, Zachariah	Gloucester	1771	8	
Son of Rebecca Row				
ROWLAND, David	Hanover	1763		298
ROWLEY, William	Stafford	1773		400
Do	of Simon Thomas			200
ROY, Peter, see Bolling, Robert Jr., Col.				
ROYSTON, Conquest	Gloucester	1770	2	200
ROYSTON, Conquest	Gloucester	1771	2	200
ROYSTON, Richard	Gloucester	1770	8	800
ROYSTON, Richard	Gloucester	1771	7	800
ROZARRO, Mary	James City	1769	1	
RUE, Peter	James City	1768	3	325
RUE, Peter	James City	1769	3	325
RUSELL, Burnal	James City	1768	1	75
RUSEL, Burnal	James City	1769	1	75
RUSSEL, Edward	Hanover	1763	(1759)	100
RUSSEL, Lucy	Gloucester	1770		
RUTHERFORD, Larkin	Buckingham	1774	1	
RUTHERFORD, Larkin, see Low, Wm.				
RYLAND, Sarah	Gloucester	1770	2	
RYLAND, Sarah	Gloucester	1771	2	
RYLIE, John	Gloucester	1770	3	150
SADDLER, John (Bro. of Thomas)	Gloucester	1770	1	260
SADDLE, John	Gloucester	1771	3	260
SADDLER, Thos.	Gloucester	1771		
SADDLER, Thomas	Gloucester	1770		
SADDLER, William	Gloucester	1770	1	
(pd. by Thomas Saddler)				
SADLER, Sarah (Kingston Par.)	Gloucester	1774		
SADLER, Sarah (Kingston Par.)	Gloucester	1775		
SADLER, Susanna (Kingston Par.)	Gloucester	1774		
SADLER, Susanna (Kingston Par.)	Gloucester	1775		
ST. MARTIN'S GLEBE	Hanover	1763		350
ST. PAUL'S GLEBE	Hanover	1763		337
SALLY, John	Buckingham	1774	1	
SALLE, see Galle, Terry				
SALLE, Hunt, see Salle, Wm. Junr.				
SALLE, Isaac	Buckingham	1774	1	
SALLE, Jacob	Buckingham	1774	2	
SALLE, John	Buckingham	1774	1	
SALLE, Olive	Buckingham	1774	1	
SALLE, William Senr.	Buckingham	1774	7	
Ayres, Mathias				
SALLE, Wm. Junr.	Buckingham	1774	2	
Salle, Hunt				
SALLEY, Jacob	Buckingham	1773	3	
Durram, James				
SALLEY, Moses	Buckingham	1773	1	
SALLEY, William Junr.	Buckingham	1773	1	
SALLEY, William Sr.	Buckingham	1773	8	
Ayres, Mathias				
SAMPSON, John (Kingston Par.)	Gloucester	1774	2	
SAMPSON, John (Kingston Par.)	Gloucester	1775	2	
SANDERS, Benjamin	Hanover	1763		150
SANDERS, Daniel	Buckingham	1773	1	
SANDERS, Daniel	Buckingham	1773	4	
SANDERS, George	Hanover	1763		400

Name	County	Year	Tithables	Acres
SANDERS, John	Hanover	1763		100
SANDERS, John	James City	1768	13	500
SANDERS, Robt., Jr.	Buckingham	1773	2	
SANDERS, Thomas	Hanover	1763		150
SANDERS, Thomas	Buckingham	1773	8	
Baber, George				
SANDERS, Thomas	Buckingame	1774	8	
Baber, George				
SANDERS, William	James City	1768	2	
SANDIGE, Gideon insolvent	Hanover	1763		72
SANDIGE, John	Hanover	1763		50
SANDURS, James	Buckingham	1774	2	
SANGUILA, Daniel, see Cary, Archibald Col.				
SAUNDERS, (_____)el	Buckingham	1774	6	
SAUNDERS, _____, see Ralls, John				
SAUNDERS, Daniel	Buckingham	1774	6	
Pamer, Nixon				
SAUNDERS, James, see Saunders, Stephen				
SAUNDERS, John	James City	1769	14	500
SAUNDERS, John, see Saunders, Stephen				
SAUNDERS, Jno., see Jamison, Alexr.				
SAUNDERS, John, see Ralls, John				
SAUNDERS, Robert	Buckingham	1773	8	
Dunham, James				
SAUNDERS, Robt.	Buckingham	1774	10	
Bristow, Thompson				
SAUNDERS, Samuel	Buckingham	1773	6	
Burnet, Griffen				
SAUNDERS, Stephen	Buckingham	1773	14	
Saunders, James				
SAUNDERS, Stephen	Buckingham	1774	16	
Saunders, John				
SAUNDERSON, Jno., see Cottrell, Benja.				
SAUNDERSON, John, see Murry, Anthony				
SAVAGE, _____, see Hansbrough, Morias				
SAVAGE, _____, see Wallace, Michael				
SAVAGE & Carr	Stafford	1773		1034
SAVAGE, Isaac, see Hansbrough, Morias				
SAVAGE, William	Stafford	1768		1034
(of James Markham)				
SCOTT, _____, see Grant, Andrew				
SCOTT, Hugh (Tillotson Par.)	Buckingham	1773	2	
Scott, Joseph				
SCOTT, Hugh (Tillotson Par.)	Buckingham	1774	2	
Scott, Joseph				
SCOTT, John	Gloucester	1770	17	300
SCOTT, John	Gloucester	1771	16	300
SCOTT, Joseph, see Scott, Hugh				
SCOTT, Thomas Col.	Gloucester	1770		
SCOTT, Thomas Col.	Gloucester	1771		
SCOTT, Thomas, Junr.*	Gloucester	1770		
SCOTT, Tom, see Wright, George				
SCOTT, Wm.	James City	1768		
SCOTT, William	Stafford	1768		730
SCOTT, William	Stafford	1773		510
SCLATER (sic) Sacheverall	James City	1768	2	171
SCRUGS, Allen, see Scrugs, James				
SCRUGS, Isham, see Scrugs, James				
SCRUGS, James (Tillotson Par.)	Buckingham	1773	4	
Scrugs, Jesse				

Name	County	Year	Tithables	Acres
Scrugs, Allen				
SCRUGS, James	Buckingham	1774	5	
Scrugs, Jesse				
Scrugs, Allen				
Scrugs, Isham				
SCRUGGS, John	Buckingham	1773	5	
SCRUGGS, John	Buckingham	1774	6	
SCRUGGS, Jno., see Scruggs, Thomas				
SCRUGGS, Theodorick	Buckingham	1774	3	
SCRUGGS, Thomas	Buckingham	1773	2	
Scruggs, Jno.				
SCRUGGS, William	Buckingham	1773	6	
Beaber, Ambros				
Baber, Thomas				
SCRUGGS, William	Buckingham	1774	7	
Beaver, Ambrose				
Beaver, Thomas				
Beaver, Edward				
SCRUGGS, Wm., see Bates, John				
SEARS, William	Gloucester	1170	10	172
SEARS, William	Gloucester	1771	10	172
SEAWELL, Benjamin	Gloucester	1770		
SEAWELL, Benjamin	Gloucester	1771	3	
SEAWELL, John	Gloucester	1770	13	525
SEAWELL, John	Gloucester	1771	15	525
SEAWELL, Joseph	Gloucester	1770	15	525
SEAWELL, Joseph	Gloucester	1771	15	525
Paid chair tax for his mother, not named. Mentioned Benjamin Seawell of Brunswick County.				
SEAY, John	Hanover	1763		439
SEDDON, Thomas	Stafford	1768		2000
SEDDON, Thomas	Stafford	1773		2300
SELDEN, Samuel	Stafford	1768		1700
SELDEN, Samuel	Stafford	1773		1700
SELDEN, Saml., Junr., see Mason, Tomson				
SELLERS, Ann (Kingston Par.)	Gloucester	1774		
SELLERS, Ann (Kingston Par.)	Gloucester	1775		
SEMPLE, James	James City	1768	3	
SHAKELFORD, Benjamin	Gloucester	1774	9	
Kingston Parish				
SHAKELFORD, Benjamin	Gloucester	1775	9	
Kingston Parish				
SHACKLEFORD, Charles	Gloucester	1770	1	
SHACKLEFORD, Charles	Gloucester	1771	1	
SHACKLEFORD, Charles, Junr.	Gloucester	1770	1	
SHACKLEFORD, Charles, Junr.	Gloucester	1771	1	
SHACKLEFORD, Cha. Sr., see Wilson, William				
SHACKLEFORD, James (Petsworth)	Gloucester	1770		75
SHACKLEFORD, James, Junr.	Gloucester	1770	1	
SHACKLEFORD, James, Junr.	Gloucester	1771	1	
SHACKLEFORD, John	Gloucester	1771	1	
SHACKLEFORD, Roger	Hanover	1763		626
SHACKLEFORD, Sarah	James City	1768	2	100
SHACKLEFORD, Sarah	James City	1769	2	100
SHACKLEFORD, William	Gloucester	1770	1	
SHACKLEFORD, William Captn.	Gloucester	1770		
SHACKLEFORD, Zachariah	Gloucester	1770	1	
SHARP, Richard	Buckingham	1773	2	
Sharp, Richard, Jr.				
SHARP, Richard	Buckingham	1774	2	

Name	County	Year	Tithables	Acres
Sharp, Richard Jr.				
SHARP, (Ro)bert	Hanover	1763		1206
SHAW, William, see Bolling, Robert, Jr. Col.				
SHELBURN, Mary	James City	1768	2	80
SHELBURN, Mary	James City	1769	2	80
SHELTON, Francis	Buckingham	1773	1	
SHELTON, Francis	Buckingham	1774	1	
SHELTON, John	Hanover	1763		481
Do				664
SHELTON, Meriwether	Hanover	1763		1220
SHEPARD, John*	Gloucester	1770		
SHEPHERD, Edward	Gloucester	1770	1	
SHEPHERD, Edward	Gloucester	1771	1	
SHEPHERD, John	James City	1768	3	75
SHEPHERD, John	James City	1769	3	75
SHEPHERD, William, see Patteson, Thomas				
SHERMER, John	James City	1768	31	1114
SHIELDS, James	James City	1768	5	250
SHIELDS, James	James City	1769	6	250
SHIPLEY, John (Kingston Parish)	Gloucester	1774	2	
SHIPLEY, John (Kingston Parish)	Gloucester	1775	2	
SHIPLEY, Joseph (Kingston Par.)	Gloucester	1774	1	
SHIPLEY, Joseph (Kingston Par.)	Gloucester	1775	1	
SHIPLEY, Ralph (Kingston Par.)	Gloucester	1774	2	
SHIPLEY, Ralph (Kingston Par.)	Gloucester	1775	2	
SHOEMAKER, James	Buckingham	1774	1	
SHOEMAKER, James, see Shoemaker, John				
SHOEMAKER, Jeremiah, see Thomas, James				
SHOEMAKER. John	Buckingham	1773	3	
Shoemaker, James				
Shoemaker, Olander				
SHOEMAKER, John	Buckingham	1773	1	
SHOEMAKER, John	Buckingham	1774	1	
SHOEMAKER, Leander	Buckingham	1774	1	
SHOEMAKER, Olander, see Shoemaker, John				
SHOMATE, William, see Stork, Jeremiah				
SHORES, John	Hanover	1763		542
Do				135
SHORES (or SHOWRES), Thomas	Hanover	1763		100
Do			(1758)	250
SHORT, John, Exrs.	Stafford	1768		1215
SHORT, John	Stafford	1773		1215
SHURLES, Robert	Gloucester	1770		
SHURLEY, Ambrose	Hanover	1763		150
Do			(1762)	204
SHURMER, John	James City	1769	22	1114
SIDNOR, Elizabeth	Hanover	1763		700
SIDNOR, Robert	Hanover	1763		200
SIMMS, Brewster	Hanover	1763		529
SIMMS, David	Hanover	1763		350
Do				139
SIMMS, Edward	Hanover	1763		139
SIMMS, James	Hanover	1763	(1757)	200
SIMMS, John (hominy)	Hanover	1763		380
SIMMS, John, Senr.	Hanover	1763		200
Do			(1757)	750
SIMMS, Matthew	Hanover	1763		650
SIMMS, Meekings	Hanover	1763	(1757)	170
SIMMS, Micajah	Hanover	1763		139
SIMMS, Richard	Stafford	1768		50

Name	County	Year	Tithables	Acres
SIMMS, Richard	Stafford	1773		50
SIMMS, Sherwood	Hanover	1763		167
SIMS, Hannah (St. Martin's)	Hanover	1770	2	133
SIMS, Mary	Hanover	1763	(1762)	230
SINGLETON, Isaac	Gloucester	1770		
SINGLETON, John (Kingston Par.)	Gloucester	1774	1	
SINGLETON, John (Kingston Par.)	Gloucester	1775	1	
SINGLETON, Joshua	Gloucester	1770	2	
SINGLETON, Joshua	Gloucester	1771	1	
SINGLETON, Richard (Kingston Par.)	Gloucester	1774	1	
SINGLETON, Richard (Kingston Par.)	Gloucester	1775	1	
SINGLETON, Richard Hunt	James City	1768	2	
SINGLETON, Richard H.	James City	1769	4	
SINGLETON, Robert	Gloucester	1770	2	
SINGLETON, Robert	Gloucester	1771	1	
SLATER, Daniel	James City	1768	2	100
SLATER, Daniel	James City	1769	2	100
SLATER, Sacheveral	James City	1769	2	
SLAUGHTER, Nathaniel	Hanover	1763		152
SMALLWOOD, William	Stafford	1768		810
SMALLWOOD, William	Stafford	1773		810
SMETHER, John Smetheir, Garratt	Buckingham	1773	2	
SMITH, _____, see Cummings, John				
SMITH, Alexr.	Buckingham	1773	2	
SMITH, Alexr.	Buckingham	1774	2	
SMITH, Augustine	Gloucester	1770	29	1200
SMITH, Augustine	Gloucester	1771	21	1200
SMITH, Bartlet	Hanover	1763		140
SMITH, Charles	Hanover	1763		212
SMITH, David (St. Martin's)	Hanover	1770	9	348
SMITH, Francis	Hanover	1763		318
SMITH, George	Hanover	1763		234
SMITH, Guliamus	Hanover	1763		162
SMITH, Henry	Buckingham	1773	2	
SMITH, Henry	Buckingham	1774	2	
SMITH, Henry	Stafford	1768		331
SMITH, Henry	Stafford	1773		131
SMITH, Henry Junr. of Joseph Jeffress	Stafford	1768		336
SMITH, Henry Junr. Do of Jos. Jeffreys	Stafford	1773		200 296
SMITH, Isaac (Kingston Parish)	Gloucester	1774	12	
SMITH, Isaac (Kingston Parish)	Gloucester	1775	12	
SMITH, James	Gloucester	1770	1	
SMITH, James	Gloucester	1771	1	
SMITH, James	Buckingham	1773	1	
SMITH, James, see Vaughan, David				
SMITH, Jas., see Lynn, John				
SMITH, James, Senr. (St.Martin's)	Hanover	1770	4	200
SMITH, James, Junr. (St. Martin's)	Hanover	1770	2	
SMITH, John	Hanover	1763		200
SMITH, John (St. Martin's)	Hanover	1770	2	150
SMITH, John	Gloucester	1770	5	133
SMITH, John	Gloucester	1771	4	133
SMITH, John (Abingdon Par.)	Gloucester	1770	1	
SMITH, John (Abingdon Par.)	Gloucester	1771	1	
SMITH, John (Northumberland)	Gloucester	1770	7	391
SMITH, John (Northumberland)	Gloucester	1771		391
SMITH, Joseph	Hanover	1763		880

Name	County	Year	Tithables	Acres
SMITH, Joseph	Stafford	1768		133
SMITH, Michael	Gloucester	1770	1	
SMITH, Michael	Gloucester	1771	1	
SMITH, N__ey, see Pryer, Edward				
SMITH, Peter (Kingston Par.)	Gloucester	1774	6	
SMITH, Peter (Kingston Par.)	Gloucester	1775	6	
SMITH, Robert	Hanover	1763		200
SMITH, Robert	Buckingham	1773	1	
SMITH, Robert	Buckingham	1773	1	
SMITH, Robert, see Jones, Josiah				
SMITH, Robt., see Bernard, John, Senr.				
SMITH, Thomas	Stafford	1768		100
SMITH, Thomas	Stafford	1773		100
SMITH, Thomas	Gloucester	1771	1	
SMITH, Thomas	Buckingham	1774	3	
Inge, Ambross				
SMITH, Thomas (Kingston Par.)	Gloucester	1774	32	
SMITH, Thomas (Kingston Par.)	Gloucester	1775	32	
SMITH, Thos., see Smith, Wm.				
SMITH, William	James City	1768	1	
SMITH, William	James City	1769	1	
SMITH, William (St. Martin's)	Hanover	1770	4	
SMITH, Wm.	Buckingham	1773	1	
SMITH, William Capt. (Kingston	Gloucester	1774		
SMITH, William Capt. Parish)	Gloucester	1775		
SMITH, William	Buckingham	1773	3	
Smith, Thomas				
Smith, Wm., Junr.				
SMITH, William Mr.	Gloucester	1770		
SMITH, William Mr.	Gllucester	1771		
SMITH, Wm. Mr.	James City	1768		
SMITH, Wm.	Buckingham	1774	2	
Smith, Thos.				
Smith, Wm., Junr.				
SMITH, Wm., see Allen, Wm. Hunt				
SNARD, John, see Taylor, Samuel				
SNEAD, Archibald	Hanover	1763		100
SNEAD, John	Hanover	1763		134
SNEAD, Samuel	Hanover	1763		100
SNEAD, William	Hanover	1763		240
SNEAD, William Junr.	Hanover	1763	(1759)	100
SNELSON, John	Hanover	1763		847
Do				478
SNELSON, John (St. Martin's)	Hanover	1770	13	
SNELSON, Nathl. (St. Martin's)	Hanover	1770	1	100
SNELSON, William (St.Martin's)	Hanover	1770	2	
SNODDY, Cary, see Snoddy, John				
SNODDY, James	Buckingham	1774	1	
SNODDY, John	Buckingham	1773	3	
Snoddy, Cary				
Snoddy, John, Junr.				
SNODDY, John Senr.	Buckingham	1774	3	
Snoddy, John Junr.				
Snoddy, Cary				
SOLES, John	Gloucester	1770	1	75
SOLES, John	Gloucester	1771	1	75
SOLESBERRY, Nathaniel	Hanover	1763		50
SOLESBERRY, Rules	Hanover	1763		150
SORRILL, Robert	Hanover	1763		62
SOUTHALL, James Mr.	James City	1768		

Name	County	Year	Tithables	Acres
SOUTHERLAND, Sarah	James City	1768	2	
SOUTHERN, James	Buckingham	1773	1	
SOUTHERN, James	Buckingham	1774	1	
SOUTHERN, James	Buckingham	1774	1	
SOUTHERN, Joseph	Buckingham	1774	1	
SOUTHERN, Reubin, see Southern, Wm.				
SOUTHERN, Samuel	Buckingham	1773	1	
SOUTHERN, Wm.	Buckingham	1773	2	
Southern, Reubin				
SOUTHERN, Wm.	Buckingham	1774	2	
Southern, Reubin				
SPALDING, Thomas, see Cox, John				
SPAN, John	Gloucester	1771	1	
SPEARS, John	Buckingham	1774	5	
SPEARS, John	Buckingham	1773		
Spears, William				
(4 Negroes of Ane Spears)				
SPEED, George	Gloucester	1771	2	
SPEED, Philip	Gloucester	1770	1	
SPEED, Philip	Gloucester	1771	1	
SPENCER, _____ (mutilated)	Buckingham	1773	1	
SPENCER, Abraham	Hanover	1763	(1757)	303
SPENCER, Charles, see Bell, Henry				
SPENCER, David	Gloucester	1770	2	
SPENCER, David	Gloucester	1771	2	
SPENCER, Francis	Buckingham	1773	5	
SPENCER, Francis	Buckingham	1774	5	
SPENCER, Francis W.	Buckingham	1773	6	
SPENCER, Francis West	Buckingham	1774	7	
Atkins, Job				
SPENCER, John	James City	1768		
SPENCER, Mancil	James City	1768	4	114
SPENCER, Mancil	James City	1769	4	114
SPENCER, Robert (Kingston Par.)	Gloucester	1774	13	
SPENCER, Robert (Kingston Par.)	Gloucester	1775	13	
SPENCER, Samuel	Buckingham	1773	9	
Worley, William				
SPENCER, Samuel	Buckingham	1774	9	
Worley, William				
SPENCER, William	Hanover	1763		100
SPENCER, William	Buckingham	1774	1	
SPOLDIN, Thomas, see Cox, John Est.				
SPOTSWOOD, Elizabeth	Gloucester	1770	3	
SPOTSWOOD, Elizabeth	Gloucester	1771	3	
(Hugh Spotswood Est. last year)				
SPRAGINS, William	James City	1768	3	150
SPRAGINS, William	James City	1769	4	150
SPRAKS, Alexander (Kingston Par.)	Gloucester	1774	6	
SPRAKS, Alexander (Kingston Par.)	Gloucester	1775	6	
SPRATLEY, Wm. Mr.	James City	1768		350
(150 Acres Gleab land)				
SPRATLEY, William	James City	1768	9	350
SPRATLEY, William	James City	1769	10	350
STACKHOUSE, James insolvent	James City	1768		
STANARD, James, see Cannon, Wm.				
STANDLEY, Archelius	Hanover	1763		30
STANDLEY, Mary	Hanover	1763		150
STANDLEY, Pleasant	Hanover	1763		50
STANDLEY, Thomas	Hanover	1763		50
STANLEY, Eleanor	Hanover	1763		200

Name	County	Year	Tithables	Acres
STANLEY, John	Hanover	1763		403
STANLEY, Mattox	Hanover	1763		70
STANLEY, Thomas	Hanover	1763		118
STANLEY, William	Hanover	1763		100
STANHOPE, Price	James City	1768	5	484
STANHOPE, Price	James City	1769	5	434
STANTON, Matthew, see Phelps, John				
STAPLES, Isaac	Buckingham	1773	1	
STAPLES, Isaac	Buckingham	1774	1	
STAPLES, Jno., see Staples, Saml.				
STAPLES, John	Buckingham	1774	1	
STAPLES, Saml.	Buckingham	1773	9	
Staples, Jno.				
STAPLES, Saml.	Buckingham	1774	9	
Coleman, David				
STARK, James, Exrs.	Stafford	1768		218
STARK, Jeremiah	Stafford	1773		130
STARKE, Aaron	Hanover	1763		160
STARKE, James Exrs.	Stafford	1773		218
STARKE, John	Hanover	1763		487
STARLE. John Junr.	Hanover	1763		200
STARKE, Richard Esqr.	James City	1768	7	
STARKE, Richard	James City	1769	7	
STATIN, William	Buckingham	1773	2	
STATON, George	Buckingham	1773	1	
STATON, George	Buckingham	1774	1	
STATON, James	Buckingham	1774	1	
STATON, John	Buckingham	1773	2	
STATON, John	Buckingham	1774	3	
Dameron, George				
STATON, Joseph, see Staton, Wm.				
STATON, Reubin	Buckingham	1773	1	
STATON, Reubin	Buckingham	1774	1	
STATON, Wm.	Buckingham	1774	3	
Staton, Joseph				
STEDER, John (Kingston Par.)	Gloucester	1774	2	
STEDER, John (Kingston Par.)	Gloucester	1775	2	
STEPHENS, John	Buckingham	1773	2	
Green, Joseph				
STEPHENS, John	Buckingham	1774	2	
Green, Joseph				
STEPHENS, Jno., see Stephens, Thomas				
STEPHENS, Thomas	Buckingham	1773	2	
Vest, George				
STEPHENS, Thomas	Buckingham	1774	4	
Stephens, Jno.				
Vest, Geo.				
STEPHENSON, Richard	Gloucester	1770	1	
STEPHENSON, Richard	Gloucester	1771	1	
STEVENS, Henry	Gloucester	1770	5	135
STEVENS, Henry	Gloucester	1771	5	135
STEVENS, William (Kingston Par.)	Gloucester	1774	4	
STEVENS, William (Kingston Par.)	Gloucester	1775	4	
STEVISON, James, see Bates, John				
STEWARD, James	Gloucester	1770		
(Thos. Booth, Overseer)				
STEWARD, William	Stafford	1773		240
STEWART, George	Hanover	1763		200
STEWART, John (Kingston Par.)	Gloucester	1774	2	
STEWART, John (Kingston Par.)	Gloucester	1775	2	

Name	County	Year	Tithables	Acres
STEWART, Joseph	Stafford	1768		281
STEWART, Mary	James City	1768		
STEWART, William (Kingston Par.)	Gloucester	1774	7	
STEWART, William (Kingston Par.)	Gloucester	1775	7	
STILL, Henry, see Still, Wm.				
STILL, Thos.	Buckingham	1773	1	
STILL, Thos.	Buckingham	1774	1	
STILL, Wm.	Buckingham	1773	5	
Still, Henry				
STILL, Wm.	Buckingham	1774	5	
Still, Hen:				
STINSON, Alexander	Buckingham	1773	10	
STINSON, Alexr., see Childress, John				
STINSON, Alexr., Junr.	Buckingham	1773		
STINSON, Alexander, Junr.	Buckingham	1774	3	
STINSON, Alexander, Senr.	Buckingham	1774	11	
Stinson, George				
Stinson, Cary				
STINSON, David	Buckingham	1773	1	
STINSON, David	Buckingham	1774	2	
Malium, James				
STINSON, George, see Stinson, Alexander, Senr.				
STINSON, John	Buckingham	1773	9	
Adcock, Edmund				
Payne, Benja.				
STINSON, John	Buckingham	1774	8	
Adcock, Edmund				
STINSON, Joseph	Buckingham	1773	1	
STINSON, Joseph	Buckingham	1774	1	
STITH, John	Stafford	1768		1114
STITH, John	Stafford	1773		1114
STITH, Judy	James City	1769	1	
STITH, Mary	James City	1769	1	
STOAKES, Moses	Gloucester	1770	1	
STOAKES, Moses	Gloucester	1771	1	
STOAKES, Robert	Gloucester	1770	1	
STOAKES, Robert	Gloucester	1771	1	
STOAKES, Robert Junr.	Gloucester	1770	1	
STOAKES, Robert Junr.	Gloucester	1771	1	
STOAKES, Thomas	Gloucester	1770	10	305
STOAKES, Thomas	Gloucester	1771	11	305
STOAKES, William	Gloucester	1770		
STOAKES, William	Gloucester	1771		
STONE, Josias	Stafford	1768		474
STONE, Josias	Stafford	1773		470
STONE, William	James City	1769	2	100
STONE, Wm. Graves	James City	1768		100
STODGILL, John	Hanover	1763		200
STORK, Jeremiah	Stafford	1768		130
(of William Shomate)				
STRANGE, Jesse, see Strange, John				
STRANGE, John	Hanover	1763		60
STRANGE, John	Buckingham	1773	2	
STRANGE, Jesse	Buckingham	1774	2	
STRIBLING, Cokely	Stafford	1768		63
STRIBLING, Cokely	Stafford	1773		63
(Now John Stuart's)				
STRINGFELLOW, Robert	Stafford	1773		117
"Said he said to K. Geo. collector"				
STREET, John	Hanover	1763		238

Name	County	Year	Tithables	Acres
STRONG, Martin	Hanover	1763		200
STUART, Charles	Stafford	1768		812
STUART, Charles	Stafford	1773		812
STUART, John	Stafford	1768		1604
STUART, John	Stafford	1773		1604
STUART, John, see Fitzhugh, William Senr.				
STUART, John, see Stribling, Cokely				
STUART, William, Revd.	Stafford	1768		3040
STUART, William, Revd.	Stafford	1773		3040
STUART, Will. Revd., see Foote, Richard				
STUBBLEFIELD, Simon	Gloucester	1770	7	350
STUBBLEFIELD, Simon	Gloucester	1771	7	350
STUBBLEFIELD, Thomas	Gloucester	1771	6	
STUBBS, James*	Gloucester	1770		
STUBBS, John	Gloucester	1770	7	606
STUBBS, John	Gloucester	1771	8	606
STUBBS, John, Junr.	Gloucester	1770	1	
STUBBS, John, Junr.	Gloucester	1771	2	
STUBBS, Lawrence	Gloucester	1770		418
STUBBS, Lawrence	Gloucester	1771		418
STUBBS, Peter	Gloucester	1770	5	163
STUBBS, Peter	Gloucester	1771	5	163
STUBBS, Thomas	Gloucester	1770	5	100
STUBBS, Thomas	Gloucester	1771	5	100
STUBBS, William	Gloucester	1770	10	300
STUBBS, William	Gloucester	1771	9	300
STUBBS, William, Junr.*	Gloucester	1770		
SUBLETT, James	Buckingham	1773	1	
SUBLETT, James	Buckingham	1774	1	
SUDDATH, Robert	Stafford	1768		75
SUMMERS, John (Kingston Par.)	Gloucester	1774	1	
SUMMERS, John (Kingston Par.)	Gloucester	1775	1	
SURTERS, Anthony Capt.	Gloucester	1771	1	
SUTTON, John	Hanover	1763		(1759) 400
SWENEY, Moses	James City	1768	1	
SWENEY, Moses	James City	1769	1	
SWENEY, William	James City	1768	1	50
SWIFT, Thomas	Hanover	1763		828
SWINEY, Thomas	Buckingham	1773	1	
SEINNEY, Thomas	Buckingham	1774	1	
SYMES, John	Hanover	1763		1050
Do				1320
Do				100
SYMMS, _____, see Whiting, John				
TABB, Edward (Kingston Par.)	Gloucester	1774	18	
TABB, Edward (Kingston Par.)	Gloucester	1775	18	
TABB, John (Kingston Par.)	Gloucester	1774	6	
TABB, John (Kingston Par.)	Gloucester	1775	6	
TABB, Susanna (Kingston Par.)	Gloucester	1774	4	
TABB, Susanna (Kingston Par.)	Gloucester	1775	4	
TABB, Toye Estate (Kingston Par.)	Gloucester	1774	19	
TABB, Toye Estate (Kingston Par.)	Gloucester	1775	19	
TABER, Joseph (Kingston Par.)	Gloucester	1774	2	
TABER, Joseph (Kingston Par.)	Gloucester	1775	2	
TALIAFERRO, Charles	James City	1768	6	
TALIAFERRO, Charles	James City	1769	7	
TALLIAFERRO, Philip	Gloucester	1771		
TALIAFERRO, Richd. Major	James City	1768	26	975

Name	County	Year	Tithables	Acres
TALIAFERRO, Richd., Major	James City	1769	26	975
TALIAFERRO, Richard	Gloucester	1770	8	415
Hunt, John				
Whiteoak, Stephen				
TALIAFERRO, Richard	Gloucester	1771	8	
Hunt, John				
Whiteoak, Stephen				
TALIAFERRO, Richard, see White, Stephen				
TALLY, Blandena	Hanover	1763	(1762)	138
TALLY, Charles	Hanover	1763		100
TALLY, David	Hanover	1763		100
TALLY, Henry	Hanover	1763		100
TALLY, John	Hanover	1763		225
TALLY, Nathaniel	Hanover	1763		185
TALLY, Micajah	Hanover	1763		50
TALLY, Nicholas	Hanover	1763		125
TALLY, William	Hanover	1763		100
TANDY, Roger	Gloucester	1771	1	
TAPSCOTT, Henry	Buckingham	1774	3	
TARPLEY, Elisabeth	James City	1768	4	100
TARPLEY, Elisabeth	James City	1769	3	100
TATE, John	Hanover	1763		162
TATE, Margaret	Hanover	1763		290
TATE, Robert	Hanover	1763	(1762)	310
TATE, Susannah	James City	1768	9	266
TATE, Susannah	James City	1769	9	266
TAYLER, Edward	James City	1769	1	
TAYLER, James	James City	1768	6	
TAYLER, James	James City	1768	3	
TAYLER, Jeremiah	James City	1769	2	
TAYLER, Rebecca	James City	1768	4	173
TAYLER, Rebecca	James City	1769	3	173
TAYLER, Richard	James City	1768	7	696
TAYLER, Richard	James City	1769	7	696
TAYLER, William Senr.	James City	1768	8	800
TAYLER, William Senr.	James City	1769	5	800
TAYLER, Wm. insolvent	James City	1768	1	
TAYLER, William Junr.	James City	1769	1	
TAYLOR, Bartlet	Hanover	1763		95
TAYLOR, Daniel	Buckingham	1773	2	
Taylor, Richd.				
TAYLOR, Daniel	Buckingham	1774	2	
Taylor, Richd., son				
TAYLOR, George	Hanover	1763		331
Do				50
TAYLOR, George	Buckingham	1774	1	
TAYLOR, Henry	Hanover	1763		50
TAYLOR (or TYLER), Henry	Hanover	1763		50
TAYLOR, James	Hanover	1763		130
TAYLOR, James	James City	1769	4	
TAYLOR, John, see Baird, Henry				
TAYLOR, Jno., see Taylor, Richard				
TAYLOR, Jno. Exrs., see Waugh, Taylor				
TAYLOR, Joseph	Buckingham	1774	3	
Robertson, James				
TAYLOR, Joshu, see Taylor, Richd. Junr.				
TAYLOR, Joshua	Buckingham	1773	1	
TAYLOR, Mary	Gloucester	1770		
TAYLOR, Mary	Gloucester	1771		
TAYLOR, Nathaniel	Gloucester	1770		

Name	County	Year	Tithables	Acres
TAYLOR, Nathaniel	Gloucester	1771	1	
TAYLOR, Richard	Buckingham	1773	5	
Taylor, Joshua				
TAYLOR, Richard	Buckingham	1774	5	
Taylor, Jno.				
TAYLOR, Richard Junr.	Buckingham	1773	3	
TAYLOR, Richd., Junr.	Buckingham	1774	6	
Taylor, Joshua				
TAYLOR, Richard, see Taylor, Samuel				
TAYLOR, Richd., see Taylor, Daniel				
TAYLOR, Samuel	Buckingham	1773	6	
TAYLOR, Samuel	Buckingham	1774	8	
Taylor, Richard				
Snord, (sic) John				
TAYLOR. Samuel, Junr., see Nicholas, John				
TAYLOR. Samuel, Junr.	Buckingham	1773	3	
Roberson, James				
TAYLOR, William	Hanover	1763		502
TAYLOR, William	Hanover	1763		1061
Do				50
TEACLE, Michael (Kingston Par.)	Gloucester	1774	1	
TEACLE, Michael (Kingston Par.)	Gloucester	1775	1	
TEAGLE. Richard	Gloucester	1770	2	75
TEAGLE, Richard	Gloucester	1771	2	75
TEAGLE, William	Gloucester	1770	4	
TEAGLE, William	Gloucester	1771	5	
TEMPLE. Samuel (St.Martin's)	Hanover	1770	10	
TEMPLETON, Robert	Hanover	1763		50
TERRELL, Richmond	James City	1768	7	264
TERRELL. Richmond	James City	1769	6	264
TERRILL, Henry	Hanover	1763		183
TERRILL, Harry	Hanover	1763		132
TERRILL, Joel	Hanover	1763 (1762)		400
TERRILL. Peter	Hanover	1763		321
TERRILL. Timothy	Hanover	1763		877
TERRY, John	Buckingham	1773	2	
Terry, Stephen				
TERRY, Stephen	Hanover	1763		399
THACKER, Benjamin	Hanover	1763 (1754)		100
THACKER, Chesley Rev'd	Hanover	1763		200
THACKER, Echo	Hanover	1763		100
THACKER, Edwin	Hanover	1763		1750
THACKER, George	Hanover	1763		100
THACKER. William	Hanover	1763 (1753)		100
THOMAS, Ann (Kingston Par.)	Gloucester	1774	2	
THOMAS, Ann (Kingston Par.)	Gloucester	1775	2	
THOMAS, Benjamin	Stafford	1768		200
THOMSS, Benjamin	Stafford	1773		200
THOMAS, Doctor (Kingston Par.)	Gloucester	1774	1	
THOMAS, Doctor (Kingston Par.)	Gloucester	1775	1	
THOMAS, George	Hanover	1763		120
THOMAS, Henry	Buckingham	1773	2	
Legan, John				
THOMAS, Henry	Buckingham	1774	1	
THOMAS, James	Buckingham	1773	4	
THOMAS, James	Buckingham	1774	5	
Shoemaker, Jeremiah				
THOMAS, James, Senr. (Kingston	Gloucester	1774	3	
THOMAS, James, Senr. Parish)	Gloucester	1775	3	
THOMAS, James, Junr. (Kingston Par)	Gloucester	1774	3	

Name	County	Year	Tithables	Acres
THOMAS, James, Junr. Kingston Parish	Gloucester	1775	3	
THOMAS, John	Hanover	1763		100
THOMAS, John	James City	1768	3	145
THOMAS, John	James City	1769	3	145
THOMAS, John Cabell, William	Buckingham	1773	4	
THOMAS, John	Buckingham	1774	3	
THOMAS, Joseph Murrel, Wilkerson	Buckingham	1774	5	
THOMAS, Mark, Senr. (Kingston	Gloucester	1774	1	
THOMAS, Mark, Senr. Parish)	Gloucester	1775	1	
THOMAS, Morgan (Kingston Par.)	Gloucester	1774	2	
THOMAS, Morgan (Kingston Par.)	Gloucester	1775	2	
THOMAS, Simon, see Rowley, William				
THOMAS, Thomas	Buckingham	1773	1	
THOMASON, Elias	Hanover	1763		66
THOMASON, John	Hanover	1763		400
THOMPSON, Charles	Gloucester	1770	1	
THOMPSON, Charles	Gloucester	1771	1	
THOMPSON, John	Hanover	1763		1436
THOMPSON, Robt. (Constable)	Buckingham	1774		
THOMPSON, William, see Kelley, Wilford				
THOMSON, Charles	Hanover	1763	(1760)	250
THOMSON, John	James City	1769		
THOMSON, Nathaniel	Hanover	1763		100
Do				342
THOMSON, Nelson	Hanover	1763		250
THOMSON, Robert	Hanover	1763	(1760)	344
THOMSON, Robt. (Constable)	Buckingham	1773	1	
THOMSON, Roger	Hanover	1763		501
THOMSON, William	Hanover	1763		853
Do				84
THOMSON, Wm., see Garrott, Charles				
THORNBURY, John	Stafford	1768		80
THORNBURY, John	Stafford	1773		80
THORNBURY, Samuel	Stafford	1768		132
THORNBURY, Samuel "now John Pead"	Stafford	1773		132
THORNHILL, Thomas (Tillotson) Thornhill, Thomas Junr. Hawkins, Garrison	Buckingham	1773	5	
THORNHILL, Thomas Thornhill, Thomas Junr.	Buckingham	1773	5	
THORNHILL, Thomas Thornhill, Thomas Junr.	Buckingham	1774	5	
THORNHILL, Thos Thornhill, Thos., Jr. Walker, David	Buckingham	1774	6	
THORNILL, William	Buckingham	1773	1	
THORNILL, William	Buckingham	1774	1	
THORNTON, Francis	Stafford	1768		750
THORNTON, Francis	Stafford	1773		750
THORNTON, John	Hanover	1763	(1759)	337
THORNTON, John (Hanover)	Gloucester	1771		
THORNTON, Richard	Hanover	1763		294
THORNTON, William	Hanover	1763		550
THORNTON (or THONTON), William	Hanover	1763		190
THORNTON, William	Gloucester	1770	8	232
THORNTON, William	Gloucester	1771	10	232

Name	County	Year	Tith-ables	Acres
THORP, Charles	Hanover	1763		70
THORP, John	Hanover	1763		65
THORP, Thomas	James City	1768	2	
THORNTON, Esther	Gloucester	1770	9	230
THORNTON, Esther	Gloucester	1771	9	230
THORNTON, Sterling	Gloucester	1770	5	230
THORNTON, Sterling	Gloucester	1771	4	230
THROCKMORTON, John Jr.*	Gloucester	1770		
THROCKMORTON, John Senr.	Gloucester	1770	3	
THROCKMORTON, John Senr.	Gloucester	1771	3	
THROCKMORTON, Robert*	Gloucester	1770		
THRUSTON, Charles M.	Gloucester	1770		1000
THRUSTON, Sarah*	Gloucester	1770		
THURMAN, Elisha	Buckingham	1774	1	
THURMAN, John	Hanover	1763		60
THURMAN, William	Hanover	1763		400
THURSTON, Elizabeth	Gloucester	1770		
THURSTON, Elizabeth	Gloucester	1771		
TIBBS, John	Buckingham	1773	1	
TIBBS, John	Buckingham	1774	1	
TILLAGE, James*	Gloucester	1770		
TILLIDGE, Thomas	Gloucester	1770	8	100
TILLIDGE, Thomas	Gloucester	1771	10	100
TIMBERLAKE, Benjamin	Hanover	1763		900
TIMBERLAKE, John	Hanover	1763		297
TIMBERLAKE, John	Gloucester	1770	6	150
TIMBERLAKE, John	Gloucester	1771	7	150
TINDAL, Benjamin Lewis, Owin	Buckingham	1773	6	
TINDALL, Benjamin Lewis, Oleun, overseer	Buckingham	1774	6	
TINSLEY, Charles	James City	1768		
TINSLEY, Cornelius	Hanover	1763		650
TINSLEY, John	Hanover	1763		200
TINSLEY, Sherwood	Hanover	1763		91
TINSLEY, Thomas	Hanover	1763		549
TINSLEY, Thomas Jun.	Hanover	1763		65
TINSLEY, William	Hanover	1763		100
TISDALE, Shirly	Hanover	1763		89
TISDALE, Thomas	Hanover	1763		50
TODD, Thomas	Gloucester	1770		
TODD, Thos.	James City	1768		
TOMKIES, Charles*	Gloucester	1770		
TOMKIES, Francis*	Gloucester	1770		
TOMPKINS, Ann	Gloucester	1770	12	1590
TOMPKINS, Ann	Gloucester	1771	14	1590
TOMPKINS, Charles, Junr.	Gloucester	1770		
TOMPKINS, Henry	Hanover	1763		432
TOMPKINS, Samuel	Gloucester	1770	4	131
TOMPKINS, Samuel	Gloucester	1771		131
"To Clerk's note, his estate by sundry - bought at the sale"				
TOMPKINS, William	Hanover	1763		550
TONEY, Charles	Buckingham	1773	3	
TONEY, Charles	Buckingham	1774	3	
TONEY, John	Buckingham	1773	4	
TONEY, John	Buckingham	1774	4	
TONEY, Wm. Toney, Wm.	Buckingham	1773	2	
TONEY, Wm., Senr. Toney, Wm. Junr.	Buckingham	1774	2	

Name	County	Year	Tithables	Acres
TOOL, Richard	Gloucester	1771		
TRAVILLION, Thomas	Hanover	1763		958
TRAVIS, Champion	James City	1769	10	
TRAVIS, Edwd. Major	James City	1768	44	1852
TRAVIS, Edward C.	James City	1769	33	1652
TREBELL, William	James City	1768	16	107
TREBELL, William	James City	1769	19	107
TRENT, Peter	Buckingham	1773	6	
Pryde, Daniel				
TRENT, Alexr., Col.	Buckingham	1774	6	
Daniel, William Pride				
TRIVILION, Stephen	James City	1768	1	215
TREVILLION, Stephen	James City	1769	1	215
TRUEHEART, Aaron	Hanover	1763		388
TRUMAN, Wm.	Buckingham	1773	1	
TRUMAN, Wm.	Buckingham	1774	1	
TUCKER, Amos	Hanover	1763		60
TUCKER, Gideon	Hanover	1763		100
TUCKER, John	Hanover	1763		166
TUCKER, Thos., see Duiguid, Mrs. Ann				
TURNER, George	Hanover	1763		210
Do				250
Do				100
Do		(1762)		233
TURNER, John	Hanover	1763		500
TURNER, Joseph	James City	1768	10	200
TURNER, Joseph	James City	1769	9	200
TURNER, Junior	James City	1768	7	684
TURNER, Junior	James City	1769	7	684
TURNER, Mary	Hanover	1763		66
TURNER, Walter	Hanover	1763		133
TURNER, William	Hanover	1763		100
TURPIN, Thomas, Col.	Buckingham	1774	6	
Harris, William				
TURPIN, Thos.	Buckingham	1773	4	
Bailey, Ben				
TURPIN, Thomas	Buckingham	1774	4	
Bailey, Benja., overseer				
TYLER, John	Hanover	1763		100
TYLER, John	James City	1768	16	750
TYLER, John	James City	1769	17	750
TYLER, Henry	Stafford	1768		300
TYLER, Henry	Stafford	1773		300
TYLER, (or TAYLOR), Henry	Hanover	1763		50
TYLER, Lewis	James City	1768		
TYLER, Lewis	James City	1769		
TYRE, Ben, see Tyree, David, Constable				
TYRE, David	Buckingham	1773	1	
TYRE, Wm.	Buckingham	1774	1	
TYREE, David, Constable	Buckingham	1774	1	
Tyre, Ben				
TYREE, Elizabeth	Hanover	1763		124
URQHART, Walter	Buckingham	1774	2	
Macrae, Christopher				
URSERY, Elizabeth	Hanover	1763		40
URY, John	Gloucester	1771	1	
USSERY, Richard	Hanover	1763		193

Name	County	Year	Tithables	Acres
VALE, William	James City	1768	2	50
VALE, William	James City	1769	2	50
VAUGHAN, David	Gloucester	1770	14	700
Smith, James				
VAUGHAN, David	Gloucester	1771	16	431
Smith, James				
VAUGHAN, Edward	Gloucester	1771	2	
"Pd. for Cathn. Haywood"				
VAUGHAN, Elkanah	Hanover	1763		50
VAUGHAN, George	Hanover	1763		233
VAUGHAN, James	Gloucester	1770	5	41
VAUGHAN, James	Gloucester	1771	5	41
VAUGHAN, John	Hanover	1763		200
VAUGHAN, William	Gloucester	1770	5	
VAUGHAN, William	Gloucester	1771	6	
VEST, Charles	Hanover	1763		300
VEST, Geo., see Stephens, Thomas				
VEST, John	Buckingham	1773	1	
VEST, John	Buckingham	1774	1	
VEST, Richd.	Buckingham	1774	1	
VIA, David	Buckingham	1774	3	
VIA, Gideon	Hanover	1763		100
VIA, Josiah	Hanover	1763		100
VIA, Robert	Hanover	1763		128
VIA, William	Hanover	1763		63
VINCENT, John	Gloucester	1771	1	
VINES, Waddy, see Cobbs, John				
VINES, William	Hanover	1763		56
VOLE, Jane	James City	1768		
WADDY, Anthony	Hanover	1763		200
WADE, Edward	Hanover	1763		245
WADE, Edward, Jun.	Hanover	1763		100
WADE, Edmund	James City	1769	2	20
"Do 20 for J. Wade"				
WADE, Henry	Hanover	1763		192
WADE, James	James City	1768		115
WADE, Jeremiah	James City	1768	1	20
WADE, Jeremiah	James City	1769	1	20
WADE, John	James City	1768	2	40
WADE, Joseph	James City	1768	6	100
WADE, Joseph	James City	1769	5	100
WADE, Martha	James City	1768	4	280
WADE, Martha	James City	1769	4	230
WADE, Robert	Hanover	1763		200
WADE, William	Hanover	1763		597
Do				264
WADE, William Jun.	Hanover	1763	(1762)	114
WAGER, Anne	James City	1768		
WAGSTAFF, John	James City	1768		
WAKEFIELD, Pleasant	James City	1768	2	
WAKEFIELD, Pleasant	James City	1769	2	
WALDIN, Lewis	Gloucester	1770	2	247
WALDIN, Lewis	Gloucester	1771	3	247
WALDREN, William	Hanover	1763		100
WALKER, Alexander	James City	1768	7	387
WALKER, Alexander	James City	1769	8	387
WALKER, Asop	Buckingham	1774	3	

Name	County	Year	Tithables	Acres
Carter, Bailey				
WALKER, Asaph, see Cary, Robert				
WALKER, David	Buckingham	1774	1	
WALKER, David, see Thornill, Thos.				
WALKER, Edward	Gloucester	1770	1	
WALKER, Edward	Gloucester	1771	1	
WALKER, Elmore	Buckingham	1773	1	
WALKER, Elmore	Buckingham	1774	1	
WALKER, Geo.	Gloucester	1770	1	
WALKER, Hugh	James City	1768		
WALKER, Hugh	Gloucester	1770		160
WALKER, James	Buckingham	1773	6	
Brooks, Thomas				
WALKER, James	Buckingham	1774	5	
Brook(s), Thomas				
WALKER, John	Hanover	1763		380
Do				518
WALKER, John	Buckingham	1773	1	
WALKER, John	Buckingham	1773	1	
WALKER, John	Buckingham	1773	5	
Hodges, Richd.				
WALKER, John	Buckingham	1774	5	
Hodges, Richd.				
WALKER, John	Buckingham	1774	1	
WALKER, John, see Walker, Thomas				
WALKER, Hancel	Gloucester	1771	1	
WALKER, Martin	Gloucester	1770		
WALKER, Mary	James City	1769		
WALKER, Michael	Gloucester	1770	1	
WALKER, Otey (Richn. Estate)	James City	1768	2	100
WALKER, Robert	Gloucester	1771	1	
WALKER, Thomas	Gloucester	1770	13	400
WALKER, Thomas	Gloucester	1771	13	400
WALKER, Thomas	Buckingham	1773	1	
WALKER, Thomas	Buckingham	1774	2	
Walker, John				
WALKER, Widow	Hanover	1763		207
WALKER, William, Exrs.	Stafford	1768		500
WALKER, William	James City	1768	3	166
WALKER, William	James City	1769	2	166
WALKER, William	Buckingham	1773	1	
WALKER, William Exrs.	Stafford	1773		500
"Property of some person in Fauquier Co. Land lies in that County"				
WALLACE, Michael	Stafford	1768		507
Do in Culpeper				2011
Do of Savage				
WALLER, Allen	Stafford	1768		400
WALLER, Benjamin Esqr.	James City	1768	13	434
also 9 tithes				
WALLER, Benjamin	James City	1769	13	434
"To 7 tithes Jas. City Parish"				
WALLER, John, son of Charles	Stafford	1768		600
WALLER, John	Stafford	1768		200
WALLER, John, see Douglass, Cathrinn				
WALLER, Sarah	Stafford	1768		200
WALLER, Thomas	Hanover	1763		274
WALLER, William	Stafford	1768		403
WALLIS, Sarah (insolvent)	James City	1768	1	
WALLS, John	James City	1768	1	50

Name	County	Year	Tithables	Acres
WALTER, Allen	Stafford	1773		400
WALTER, John	Stafford	1773		200
WALTER, Sarah	Stafford	1773		200
WALTER, William	Stafford	1768		200
WALTER, William	Stafford	1773		200
WALTER, William	Stafford	1773		403
Do of Wm. Allen				462
WALTON, Edward	Hanover	1763		300
WALTON, John	Hanover	1763		1046
WARBURTON, Frances	James City	1768	14	715
"Paid by your son John"				
WARBURTON, Francis	James City	1769	15	715
WARBURTON, John	James City	1768	4	100
WARBURTON, John	James City	1769	3	100
WARBURTON, John, see Warburton, Frances				
WARINGTON, John	James City	1769	2	
WARRINGTON, John	James City	1768	5	
WARRIN, Wm.	Buckingham	1773	1	
WARTERS, Charles	Buckingham	1774	1	
WASH, Thomas (St. Martin's)	Hanover	1770	6	393
WASH, William (St. Martin's)	Hanover	1770	6	323
WASHER, Kirby	James City	1768	1	
WASHER, Kirby	James City	1769	1	
WASHER, Richard	Gloucester	1770	1	
WASHER, Richard	Gloucester	1771	1	
WASHER, William	Gloucester	1770	1	
"Levy in 1768 now due"				
WASHINGTON, Bailey	Stafford	1768		1200
WASHINGTON, Bailey	Stafford	1773		1200
WASHINGTON, John	Stafford	1768		490
WASHINGTON, John	Stafford	1773		490
WASHINGTON, John, Exrs	Stafford	1768		1150
WASHINGTON, Jno. Exors., see Munro, Margaret				
WASHINGTON, Jno., Exors., see Washington, Nathaniel				
WASHINGTON, Lawrence	Stafford	1768		777
WASHINGTON, Lawrence	Stafford	1773		777
WASHINGTON, Nathaniel	Stafford	1768		628
(of John Hooe)				
WASHINGTON, Nathaniel	Stafford	1773		628
Do of Jno. Washington Exrs.				
WASHINGTON, Peter	Stafford	1773		84
WASHINGTON, Robert	Stafford	1768		576
WASHINGTON, Robert	Stafford	1773		576
WASHINGTON, Samuel	Stafford	1768		1800
WASHINGTON, Townshend	Stafford	1768		600
WASHINGTON, Townshend	Stafford	1773		600
WASHINGTON, Warner	Gloucester	1770		1838
WASHINGTON, Warner	Gloucester	1771		1838
WATERFORD, Adam	James City	1769	2	
WATKINS, Edward	Hanover	1763		67
WATKINS, Joel	Buckingham	1773	1	
WATKINS, Joel	Buckingham	1774	2	
Naile, Wm.				
WATKINS, John, see Winston, Anthony				
WATKINS, Margaret	Hanover	1763		67
WATLINGTON, Paul	Gloucester	1770	4	
WATLINGTON, Paul	Gloucester	1771	3	
WATLINGTON, Paul Junr.	Gloucester	1771	4	
WATLINGTON, Rowland	Gloucester	1770	4	
WATLINGTON, Richard	Gloucester	1771	3	

Name	County	Year	Tithables	Acres
WATLINTON, William	Gloucester	1770	2	
WATLINTON, William	Gloucester	1771	2	
WATSON, John	Hanover	1763		1413
WATSON, Jonathan, Majr.	Gloucester	1771	16	1838
WATT, William	Buckingham	1773	11	
Dean, Richd.				
WATT, William	Buckingham	1774	11	
Dean, Richd.				
WATTERFOOT, Adam	James City	1768	2	
WATTS, James	Hanover	1763		125
WAUGH, _____, see Monk, _____				
WAUGH, Gowrey	Stafford	1768		1570
WAUGH, Gowrey	Stafford	1773		1570
WAUGH, James	Stafford	1768		1000
WAUGH, James	Stafford	1773		1000
(lives in Fairfax)				
WAUGH, John	Stafford	1768		1700
WAUGH, John, Exrs.	Stafford	1773		1700
WAUGH, Joseph Exrs.	Stafford	1768		504
WAUGH, Joseph	Stafford	1773		504
WAUGH, Taylor	Stafford	1768		714
Do of Taylor, Jno. Exrs 200 and 157 Acres				
WEAKLAND, Wm. K.	Buckingham	1773	5	
WEAKLAND, Wm. K.	Buckingham	1774	5	
WEATHERS, John	James City	1768	1	196½
WEATHERS, John	James City	1769	3	196½
WEAVER, Daniel	Buckingham	1773	1	
WEAVER, Daniel	Buckingham	1774	1	
WEBB, Foster	Hanover	1763		230
WEBB, George Jun.	Hanover	1763	(1757)	687
WEBB, John	Hanover	1763		100
WEBB, John	Buckingham	1774	2	
WEBB, Julius	Hanover	1763		100
WEBB, Martin	Buckingham	1773	1	
WEBB, Martin	Buckingham	1774	1	
WEBB, Samuel	Buckingham	1773	1	
WEBB, Theodrick	Buckingham	1773	11	
Garratt, John				
WEBB, Theodorick	Buckingham	1774	14	
Radford, John				
Fitchjawald (sic), John				
WEBB, William	Hanover	1763		100
WEBB, Wm.	Buckingham	1773	4·	
Francis, Wm.				
WEBB, Wm.	Buckingham	1774	3	
WELCH, (Ja)mes	Buckingham	1774	1	
WELDON, Benjamin	James City	1768	12	210
WELDON, Benjamin	James City	1769	12	210
WELLS, Carty	Stafford	1768		468
WELLS, Cartey	Stafford	1773		450
WELMAN, Matthew	Hanover	1763		290
WELSH, James	Buckingham	1773	1	
WEST, Edward (of Wm. Mills)	Stafford	1768		100
WEST, Edwd.	Stafford	1773		100
WEST, Edward, see Withers, John				
WEST, James (Petsworth Par.)	Gloucester	1771	1	
WEST, John (Abingdon Par.)	Gloucester	1770	2	
WEST, John (Abingdon Par.)	Gloucester	1771	3	
WEST, Mary	Gloucester	1770	3	192
WEST, Mary	Gloucester	1771	2	192

Name	Company	Year	Tith-ables	Acres
WEST, Richard	Buckingham	1773	3	
WEST, Richard	Buckingham	1774	4	
WEST, Thomas	Gloucester	1770	3	
WEST, Thomas	Gloucester	1771	3	
WEST, William	Gloucester	1770	1	37
WEST, William	Gloucester	1771		37
WEST, William (Abingdon Par.)	Gloucester	1770	1	
WEST, William (Abingdon Par.)	Gloucester	1771	1	
WEST, William (of Col. Cocke)	Stafford	1768		110
WEST, Wm. (of Cocke)	Stafford	1773		110
WESTCOMB, Nicholas (Kingston Par.)	Gloucester	1774	8	
WESTCOMB, Nicholas (Kingston Par.)	Gloucester	1775	8	
WESTON, Major (Kingston Par.)	Gloucester	1774	5	
WESTON, Major (Kingston Par.)	Gloucester	1775	5	
WEVER, John	Buckingham	1773	1	
WEVER, (J)ohn	Buckingham	1774	1	
WHARTON, Edward	Hanover	1763	(1762)	90
WHEELER, _____, see Price, Thomas				
WHEELER, Anne	Hanover	1763		100
WHEELER, Benjamin	Buckingham	1774	1	
WHEELER, Charles	Buckingham	1774	2	
Wheeler, John, son				
WHEELER, Mark	Hanover	1763		150
WHEELER, Robert	Hanover	1763		150
WHEELER, William	Stafford	1768		100
WHEELER, William	Stafford	1773		100
WHEELER, William (of Thos.Price)	Stafford	1768		100
WHELER, Archer	Buckingham	1774	1	
WHELER, Charles	Buckingham	1773	2	
Wheler, Joe				
WHELER, Sary	Buckingham	1774	1	
WHICKER, Benjamin	Hanover	1763		100
WHICKER, James	Hanover	1763		200
WHITE, Abram	Gloucester	1771	1	
WHITE, Barret	Hanover	1763		311
WHITE, Catharine	Gloucester	1770		
WHITE, Edward (Kingston Par.)	Gloucester	1774	1	
WHITE, Edward (Kingston Par.)	Gloucester	1775	1	
WHITE, Elias	Hanover	1763		60
WHITE, Henry (Tillotson Par.)	Buckingham	1773	2	
White, Henry Page				
WHITE, Henry (Tillotson Par.)	Buckingham	1774	2	
White, Henry Page				
WHITE, James	Hanover	1763		463
WHITE, James (Kingston Par.)	Gloucester	1774	1	
WHITE, James (Kingston Par.)	Gloucester	1775	1	
WHITE, James (Kingston Par.)	Gloucester	1774	1	
WHITE, James (Kingston Par.)	Gloucester	1775	1	
WHITE, James Junr. (Kingston Par.)	Gloucester	1774	2	
WHITE, James Junr. (Kingston Par.)	Gloucester	1775	2	
WHITE, John	Hanover	1763	(1762)	100
WHITE, John (Petsworth Par.)	Gloucester	1770	1	
WHITE, John (Kingston Par.)	Gloucester	1774	1	
WHITE, John (Kingston Par.)	Gloucester	1775	1	
WHITE, John (Kingston Par.)	Gloucester	1774	1	
WHITE, John (Kingston Par.)	Gloucester	1775	1	
WHITE, John (Kingston Par.)	Gloucester	1774	1	
WHITE, John (Kingston Par.)	Gloucester	1775	1	
WHITE, John (Tillotson Par.)	Buckingham	1773	1	
WHITE, John (Tillotson Par.)	Buckingham	1773	1	

Name	County	Year	Tithables	Acres
WHITE. John (Tillotson Par.)	Buckingham	1774	1	
WHITE, John Junr. (Kingston Par.)	Gloucester	1774	1	
WHITE, John Junr. (Kingston Par.)	Gloucester	1775	1	
WHITE, John, see Bryant, Isaac				
WHITE, Joseph	Gloucester	1770	1	
WHITE, Joseph	Gloucester	1771	1	
WHITE, Richard (Kingston Par.)	Gloucester	1774	2	
WHITE, Richard (Kingston Par.)	Gloucester	1775	2	
WHITE, Samuel	Hanover	1763		100
WHITE, William (Kingston Par.)	Gloucester	1774	1	
WHITE, William (Kingston Par.)	Gloucester	1775	1	
WHITE, William Senr. Kingston Parish	Gloucester	1774	2	
WHITE, William Senr. Kingston Parish	Gloucester	1775	2	
WHITEFOOT, Cotton	Stafford	1768		400
WHITEING, John	Stafford	1768		100
WHITELOCK. David	Hanover	1763		470
WHITELOCK, Matthew	Hanover	1763		229
WHITE(S), Stephen	Gloucester	1770	1	
WHITE(S). Stephen 1771 Levy paid by Richard Taliaferro	Gloucester	1771	1	
WHITEOAK, Stephen, see Taliaferro, Richard				
WHITING, Capt., see Hall, John				
WHITING, Francis	Gloucester	1770	37	1200
WHITING, Francis	Gloucester	1771	40	1200
WHITING, Henry	Gloucester	1770		446
WHITING, John	Gloucester	1770	7	383
			Mrs. Bushrod	1280
WHITING, John	Gloucester	1771	7	War Par.
Do			12	Petsworth
Do				383
Do			Symmes Land	148
Do			Iveson Est.	326
Do			Bushrod's Land	1200
WHITING, John Now Thos. Bunbury's	Stafford	1773		100
WHITING, Mary	Gloucester	1770	8	
WHITING, Mary (Mother of Peter B.)	Gloucester	1771	8	
WHITING, Peter, see Davis, John, overseer				
WJOTOMG, Peter B., see Whiting, Mary				
WHITING, Peter Beverly	Gloucester	1770	46	1850
WHITING, Peter Beverly Pd. mother's levy	Gloucester	1771	45	1850
WHITING, Thomas	Gloucester	1770	63	1770
WHITING, Thomas	Gloucester	1771	63	1770
WHITLEY, _____, see Knox, John				
WHITNEY, Jeremiah Bauldock, Richard	Buckingham	1773	11	
WHITNEY, Jeremiah Bauldock, Richard	Buckingham	1774	11	
WHITTON, John (St. Martin's)	Hanover	1770	3	100
WIATT, Edward, Junr.	Gloucester	1770	8	1038
WIATT, Edward, Junr.	Gloucester	1771	6	1038
WIATT. John	Gloucester	1770	6	332
WIATT, John	Gloucester	1771	7	332
WIAT, Captn. John	Gloucester	1770		333
WIATT, Peter	Gloucester	1770	9	332
			Geo. Naughton	815

Name	County	Year	Tithables	Acres
WIATT, Peter	Gloucester	1771	11	332
	Geo. Naughton			815
WIATT, William	Gloucester	1770	1	
WIATT, William	Gloucester	1771		
WIDDERBURN, Alexander	Gloucester	1771	7	700
WIGGENTON, P., see Bales, Yearls				
WIGGINGTON, Henry, Exrs.	Stafford	1768		50
WIGGINGTON, James, Exr.	Stafford	1768		100
WIGGINGTON, Peter	Stafford	1768		84
WIGGINTON, Henry	Stafford	1773		50
WIGGINTON, James	Stafford	1773		100
WILD, Thomas	Hanover	1763		500
WILKENSON, Major	Buckingham	1773	1	
WILKERSON, Turner, see Wilkerson, Wm.				
WILKERSON, William	Buckingham	1773	3	
WILKERSON, Wm.	Buckingham	1774	5	
Wilkerson, Turner				
WILKINS, Samuel	James City	1768	5	208
WILKINS, Samuel	James City	1769	5	208
WILKINSON, Cary	James City	1768	8	100
WILKINSON, Cary	James City	1769	9	100
WILKINSON, Edward	James City	1768	5	
WILKINSON, Edward	James City	1769	5	
WILKISON, Joseph Thomas	Buckingham	1773		
WILLIAMS, _____, see Knox, John				
WILLIAMS, Benjamin	Stafford	1768		225
Do				136
WILLIAMS, Benjamin	Stafford	1773		225
Do				136
WILLIAMS, Daniel (Kingston Par.)	Gloucester	1774	9	
WILLIAMS, Daniel (Kingston Par.)	Gloucester	1775	9	
WILLIAMS, Dudley	James City	1768	3	340
WILLIAMS, Dudley	James City	1769	2	340
WILLIAMS, Dudley	James City	1769	3	110
WILLIAMS, George	Stafford	1768		196
Do				136
WILLIAMS, Hugh	James City	1768		
WILLIAMS, Jacob	Hanover	1763		140
WILLIAMS, Johanna	Gloucester	1770		
WILLIAMS, John	Hanover	1763		280
WILLIAMS, John	Gloucester	1770	9	418
WILLIAMS, John	Gloucester	1771	8	418
WILLIAMS, John, see Jones, Josiah				
WILLIAMS, John, see Low, William				
WILLIAMS, Nathaniel	Hanover	1763		80
WILLIAMS, Nathaniel	Stafford	1768		1542
WILLIAMS, Nathaniel	Stafford	1773		1406
WILLIAMS, Richard	Buckingham	1773	1	
WILLIAMS, Richard	Buckingham	1774	1	
WILLIAMS, Robt.	Buckingham	1774	4	
Gowing, Wm.				
WILLIAMS, Rubin, see Ruton, John				
WILLIAMS, Thomas (Kingston Par.)	Gloucester	1774	2	
WILLIAMS, Thomas (Kingston Par.)	Gloucester	1775	2	
WILLIAMS, Timothy	Hanover	1763	(1762)	100
WILLIAMS, William	Stafford	1768		200
WILLIAMS, William	Stafford	1773		200
WILLIAMS, Wm., Estate	James City	1768		
WILLIAMSON, Allice	James City	1768		
WILLIAMSON, John	Hanover	1763		550

Name	County	Year	Tith-ables	Acres
WILLIAMSON, Martha	Hanover	1763		187
WILLIAMSON, Thomas	Buckingham	1774	1	
WILLIAMSON, Walter	Stafford	1768		146
WILLIAMSON, Walter	Stafford	1773		146
WILLIAMSON, William	Buckingham	1773	4	
WILLIAMSON, William	Buckingham	1774	4	
WILLIS, Ann (Kingston Par.)	Gloucester	1774		
WILLIS, Ann (Kingston Par.)	Gloucester	1775		
WILLIS, Francis, see Willis, Robert C.				
WILLIS, Francis, Junr.	Gloucester	1770	29	1500
WILLIS. Francis, Junr.	Gloucester	1771	28	1500
WILLIS. Francis, Senr.	Gloucester	1770		2800
WILLIS, Francis, Senr.	Gloucester	1771	38	2800
WILLIS, Henry (Kingston Par.)	Gloucester	1774	2	
WILLIS, Henry (Kingston Par.)	Gloucester	1775	2	
WILLIS, James (Kingston Par.)	Gloucester	1774	1	
WILLIS, James (Kingston Par.)	Gloucester	1775	1	
WILLIS, John (Kingston Par.)	Gloucester	1774	1	
WILLIS, John (Kingston Par.)	Gloucester	1775	1	
WILLIS, John (Kingston Par.)	Gloucester	1774	18	
WILLIS, John (Kingston Par.)	Gloucester	1775	18	
WILLIS, Mesheck Jones, Jno.	Buckingham	1774	2	
WILLIS, Richard (Kingston Par.)	Gloucester	1774	1	
WILLIS, Richard (Kingston Par.)	Gloucester	1775	1	
WILLIS, Robert C.	Gloucester	1770	30	
WILLIS, Robert C.	Gloucester	1771	9	
WILLIS, Stephen	Hanover	1763		900
WILLIS, Thomas (Kingston Par.)	Gloucester	1774	1	
WILLIS, Thomas (Kingston Par.)	Gloucester	1775	1	
WILLIS, William (Kingston Par.)	Gloucester	1774	1	
WILLIS, William (Kingston Par.)	Gloucester	1775	1	
WILLIS, William (Kingston Par.)	Gloucester	1774	3	
WILLIS, William (Kingston Par.)	Gloucester	1775	3	
WILSON, Mary	Hanover	1763		(1762) 127
WILSON, Thomas	James City	1768		
WILSON. Thomas Mr.	James City	1768		
WILSON, Thomas*	Gloucester	1770		
WILSON, William (Abingdon Par.)	Gloucester	1770	1	
WILSON, William Pd. Cha. Shackleford's Sr. Tithes	Gloucester	1771	1	
WINDER, John (Kingston Par.)	Gloucester	1774	2	
WINDER, John (Kingston Par.)	Gloucester	1775	2	
WINDER, Thomas (Kingston Par.)	Gloucester	1774	3	
WINDER, Thomas (Kingston Par.)	Gloucester	1775	3	
WINFREE, George	Buckingham	1773	1	
WINFREE, George	Buckingham	1774	1	
WINGO, John	Buckingham	1774	1	
WINKFIELD, John	Hanover	1763		(1762) 350
WINKFIELD, John, Jun.	Hanover	1763		375
WINKFIELD, Mary	Hanover	1763		365
WINKFIELD, Thomas	Hanover	1763		474
WINNE, John	Hanover	1763		1180
Do				400
WINSTON, Anthony	Hanover	1763		1259
Do				529
WINSTON, Anthony Winston, Anthony, Jr. Watkins, John	Buckingham	1773	34	
WINSTON, Barbra	Hanover	1763		1743

Name	County	Year	Tith-ables	Acres
WINSTON, Barbra	Hanover	1763		400
Do			(1759)	317
WINSTON, Geddes	Hanover	1763		330
WINSTON, Isaac	Hanover	1763		1150
Do			(1762)	100
WINSTON, Isaac, Jun.	Hanover	1763	(1753)	300
WINSTON, James	Hanover	1763		734
WINSTON, John	Hanover	1763		75
WINSTON, John	Gloucester	1770	1	
WINSTON, Mary	Hanover	1763		270
WINSTON, Mary	Hanover	1763		172
WINSTON, William	Hanover	1763		550
Do				200
Do			(1762)	441
WINSTON, William, Jun.	Hanover	1763	(1753)	1076
WINSTONE, Anthony	Buckingham	1774	33	
Winston, Antho. Jur.				
Balkins (or Batkins), John				
Boyle, Wm.				
WISE, John (returned Insolvent)	James City	1768	1	
WISE, John	Gloucester	1770		
WISE, John	Gloucester	1771		
WISHART, _____ Exrs., see Grigg, John				
WITHERS, _____, see Jefferys, John				
WITHERS, Elizabeth, see Withers, John				
WITHERS, Elizth, see Mercer, George				
WITHERS, Cain	Stafford	1768		460
WITHERS, James	Stafford	1773		100
WITHERS, John	Stafford	1768		600
Do	of Welch			496
"Arrs. (Arrears) from Fauquier Rental" of Elizabeth Withers				400
WITHERS, John	Stafford	1773		1496
Do	of Edward West			100
WITT, Ben	Buckingham	1773		
Witt, Ben, Junr.				
WOOD, _____, see Peters, James				
WOOD, Henry	Hanover	1763		175
WOOD, Nehe. (Nehemiah)	Stafford	1773		200
(of Crosby)				
WOOD, Rachell	Gloucester	1770	7	700
WOOD, Rachell	Gloucester	1771	7	858
WOOD, Rachel, see Wood, Wm., Estate				
WOOD, Thomas	Buckingham	1773	2	
WOOD, Thomas	Buckingham	1774	1	
WOOD, Thos., see Johns, William				
WOOD, Wm., Estate	Gloucester	1770	3	
Rachel Wood paid levy				
WOOD, Wm., Estate	Gloucester	1771	3	
Rachel Wood paid levy				
WOODALL, David	Buckingham	1773	1	
WOODALL, David	Buckingham	1774	1	
WOODALL, James	Buckingham	1773	1	
WOODALL, William	Buckingham	1773	1	
WOODALL, William	Buckingham	1774	1	
WOODEN, George (Kingston Par.)	Gloucester	1774	1	
WOODEN, George (Kingston Par.)	Gloucester	1775	1	
WOODFOLK, Joseph	Hanover	1763		634
WOODSON, Anderson, see Bolling, Archibald				
WOODSON, Jacob	Buckingham	1773	4	

Name	County	Year	Tithables	Acres
WOODSON, Jacob	Buckingham	1774	5	
Buxston, George				
WOODSON, Jesse, see Woodson, William				
WOODSON, John	Buckingham	1774	7	
Wm., Alexr. (sic)				
WOODSON, John, see Gannaway, John, Jr.				
WOODSON, Shadrack	Buckingham	1773	4	
WOODSON, Tucker	Buckingham	1773	1	
WOODSON, William	Buckingham	1773	3	
Woodson, Jesse				
WOODSON, William	Buckingham	1774	4	
Woodson, Jesse				
WOODWARD, Chesley	James City	1769		
WOODWARD, Jeremiah, see Epperson, Littleberry				
WOODWARD, John	James City	1769	1	
WOODWARD, Randolph	James City	1768		
WOODY, John	Hanover	1763		80
WOODY, Martha	Hanover	1763		170
WOODY, Micajah	Hanover	1763		200
WOODY, Samuel	Hanover	1763		120
WOOLDRIDGE, Henry	Buckingham	1773	3	
WOOLDRIDGE, Henry	Buckingham	1774	3	
WORD, Peter, see Curd, William				
WORLEY, John, see Benning, John				
WORLEY, John, Miller, see Benning, Jno.				
WORLEY, Wm., see Spencer, Samuel				
WORMLY, John Mr.	James City	1768		
WORMLEY, Ralph	Gloucester	1770		60
WRAY, Mary	James City	1768	3	100
WRAY, Mary	James City	1769	3	100
WRIGHT, Augustine	Buckingham	1774	1	
WRIGHT, George	Buckingham	1773	4	
Perkins, Henry				
Scott, Tom				
WRIGHT, Jane	Gloucester	1770	1	
WRIGHT, John	Gloucester	1770	1	
WRIGHT, John	Buckingham	1773	2	
Wright, Thos.				
WRIGHT, Petr.	Buckingham	1774	1	
WRIGHT, Randolph	Buckingham	1773	1	
WRIGHT, Randolph	Buckingham	1774	1	
WRIGHT, Richard	Gloucester	1770	1	253
WRIGHT, Richard	Gloucester	1771	1	253
WRIGHT, Richard	Hanover	1763		130
WRIGHT, Richard (St. Martin's)	Hanover	1770	3	205
WRIGHT, Thomas (Tillotson Par.)	Buckingham	1773	4	
WRIGHT, Thomas	Buckingham	1773	1	
WRIGHT, Thomas	Buckingham	1774	4	
WRIGHT, Thomas	Gloucester	1770	5	253
WRIGHT, Thomas, see Burk, George				
WRIGHT, Thos., see Wright, John				
WYATT, Joseph	James City	1768		
WYTHE, Henry	Hanover	1763	(1757)	133
WYTHE, Mary	James City	1768		
YANCEY, Hannah	Hanover	1763	(1758)	100
YANCEY, John	Stafford	1773		400
YANCEY, John, Junr.	Stafford	1768		400
YANCY, Mary (St. Martin's)	Hanover	1770	8	275

Name	County	Year	Tith-ables	Acres
YANCEY, William	Hanover	1763	(1758)	100
YARBURROW, Alsup	Hanover	1763		250
YATEMAN, Thomas	Gloucester	1770		60
YATES, Mary	Gloucester	1770	12	250
Pd. by William Massey				
YATES, Mrs., see Massey, Robert Mr.				
YATES, Robert	Stafford	1768		550
YATES, Robert	Stafford	1773		550
YEAMONS, Charles	Hanover	1763		254
YEATMAN, Dickison (insolvent)	James City	1768	2	
YOUNG, William	Stafford	1768		75
Bot (sic) of John Addison				
YOUNG, William, Exrs.	Stafford	1773		75
"now Townshend Dade's"				

www.ingramcontent.com/pod-product-compliance
Lightning Source LLC
Chambersburg PA
CBHW020658300426
44112CB00007B/437